Welcome to
iPad
Tips, Tricks, Apps & Hacks

I f you think you know everything your iPad has to offer, think again. It is the tablet that keeps on giving, and it now has so many uses that it almost makes every other gadget redundant. From the basic functions that come built-in – such as the contacts, calendar and internet – to the added extras available through the App Store, your iPad opens up a whole new world of usability and functionality. In this book we will be showing you how to get even more from your iPad. Starting off with the top 100 tips and tricks to help you in your everyday life, there's then a wealth of tutorials showing you how to dictate notes, create comics and build your own app. You can also learn about jailbreaking, showing you the benefits, how to do it, and guides that will help you extend the functions of your iPad. On top of all that we round up all the latest and greatest apps from the App Store.

iPad
Tips, Tricks, Apps & Hacks

Imagine Publishing Ltd
Richmond House
33 Richmond Hill
Bournemouth
Dorset BH2 6EZ
☎ +44 (0) 1202 586200
Website: www.imagine-publishing.co.uk

Editor in Chief
Aaron Asadi

Production Editor
Jon White

Design
Charles Goddard

Printed by
William Gibbons, 26 Planetary Road, Willenhall, West Midlands, WV13 3XT

Distributed in the UK & Eire by
Imagine Publishing Ltd, www.imagineshop.co.uk. Tel 01202 586200

Distributed in Australia by
Gordon & Gotch, Equinox Centre, 18 Rodborough Road, Frenchs Forest,
NSW 2086. Tel + 61 2 9972 8800

Distributed in the Rest of the World by
Marketforce, Blue Fin Building, 110 Southwark Street, London, SE1 0SU

IMAGINE
PUBLISHING

Contents

Everything you need to get the most from your iPad & iPad 2

64 World news on the go

156 Become an iPad DJ

128 View movies with ease

Essential iPad
Tips&Tricks

Get more from your iPad by digging deeper into its default apps and unleash the extra features in its operating system

Like the iPhone before it, the iPad is an incredibly versatile device that can enhance your life in many different ways. If you fancy a trip to the cinema, you can use your iPad to discover the time and location of the next bus, watch a trailer to see what film looks good and even make a cinema booking. Your iPad empowers you by giving quick access to information. Indeed, if you leave home without it you'll feel cut off from the rest of the world!

All iPads behave identically when you first get them out of the box, but that's no reason for us to use our gadgets in the same way as everyone else. By reading our tips you'll be able to change the way the default apps and the operating system behave, to make them suit your particular needs. You'll also discover ways to squeeze more functionality out of the default apps and become an iPad expert!

01

Which direction am I travelling in?

When using the Maps app, you can see your current position on the map as a blue dot. If you're unsure which direction you are walking in, simply tap on the compass arrow icon on the top bar. A torchlight-style beam will emit from the blue location dot, indicating your current direction. So you need never get lost again.

03

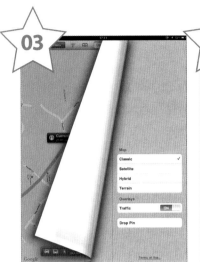

04

05

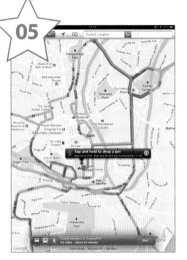

02

Share your location

If you want to rendezvous with a friend, tap the 'i' icon by the pin that indicates your current location. Tap the 'Share Location' button and then email or MMS a map reference to your friend. They can tap the map's URL link and view your location as a pin in their own Maps app.

03

Drop a pin

If you can't find a precise location via the Maps app's handy search option, you can tap on the curled paper at the bottom right and press 'Drop Pin'. You can then drag the pin to a point on the map (or just tap and hold on the screen), tap the blue 'i' icon and click on the 'Directions to Here button'.

04

Get bus times

By default, the Maps app's Directions function displays the route and time it'll take you to get to your destination when travelling by car. If you click the Bus icon you'll get walking directions to the nearest bus stop, then see the relevant bus number and departure time to take you to your destination.

05

Instant traffic report

If you're not sure what route to take, tap the Maps app's curled paper (at the bottom right) and toggle the Traffic button on. Clear roads will be marked with green, slow moving traffic will appear as amber and real snarl ups will be highlighted by flashing red lines. You can then plan a faster route.

06

Give turn-by-turn driving directions

The Maps app's Directions menu displays routes as a line from A to B, but this is not suitable for a driver to access safely while on the move. Tap 'Directions' at the top of the window then tap 'Start' in the directions bar. Now tap the list icon in the blue bar for turn-by-turn directions.

07

Pause your downloads

If you're trying to update a bunch of apps at the same time and don't feel like waiting forever for one of them to finish, it's possible to pause the installation of an app and form your own orderly queue. Simply tap an app icon while it is downloading to pause the process. Tap it again to resume.

08

Create big print

If you don't always have your reading glasses to hand, it can be a hassle having to squint to read small fonts within text messages, notes or emails. Pop into Settings>General and scroll down to Accessibility. Then use the Large Text option to make the words in many applications look larger.

09

Perform a double-tap zoom

For a closer look at your app icons, turn on the 'Zoom' option in the Accessibility menu. A double tap with three fingers will then magnify a part of the screen. You can scroll around the zoomed screen by dragging with three fingers. Double-tap with three fingers to zoom out again.

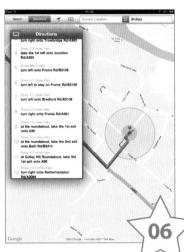

06

08

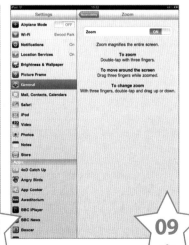

09

10 Activate VoiceOver

You can get your iPad to read out the contents of any screen (including button labels) by turning on the 'VoiceOver' option (in Accessibility). This will dramatically change the way you interact with the iPad, but is handy for listening to a book while on the move.

11 Avoid problematic auto-corrections

Your iPad corrects misspelled words when you type, but it can get it wrong. To avoid missing auto-corrected words, go to Settings>General>Accessibility. Turn 'Speak Auto-text' on and you'll hear a voice pronounce every corrected word.

12 Fully close paused or open apps

Double-click the Home button to show the app switcher. Swipe to scroll left or right to see all currently open apps. To quit an app, hold a finger on its icon for a few seconds until it starts to wiggle, then click the red circle icon.

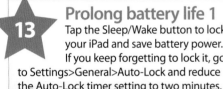

13 Prolong battery life 1

Tap the Sleep/Wake button to lock your iPad and save battery power. If you keep forgetting to lock it, go to Settings>General>Auto-Lock and reduce the Auto-Lock timer setting to two minutes. If you don't need the Bluetooth or Wi-Fi functions, turn those Settings off.

14 Enjoy quieter typing

If you have grown to dislike that clicking sound that occurs every time you hit a letter on the keyboard then there is a simple solution to enjoy quiet typing. Go to Settings>General> Sounds and then move the 'Keyboard Clicks' slider to 'Off'.

15 Fetch not push

Your iPad regularly chats to the server to find the latest Push Notifications, like Facebook updates. This can increase the demands on your battery. Go to Settings>Mail, Contacts, Calendars and turn Push off. You can then fetch data according to a less frequent schedule.

16 Rearrange your icons

If you fancy tidying up your home screen and moving some icons around, tap and hold on any icon until all of the icons start to shake (jiggle mode) and then press and hold on a moving icon. You will then be able to drag and arrange it wherever you want on the screen.

17 Playback control

To start or stop audio from radio apps (like TuneIn Radio), you usually need to click on their icons and then use their playback controls. Alternatively, double-tap Home and swipe to the far left of the app switcher to access playback controls for the active audio app.

18 Personalise the screen

On iPads running iOS 4, you can personalise your Home screen to display your favourite photo. Choose Settings>Brightness & Wallpaper. Browse to your iPad's Photo Library and pick a shot. You can assign one shot to the Lock screen and a different one to the Home screen.

17

18

19

Use categorised folders to store your apps

You could spread many apps across 11 scrollable screens, which means lots of finger swiping to find specific ones. Alternatively, hold your finger on an app to make it wiggle, then drag it onto another app to create a folder. Label your folders to store apps by category (like Navigation, Photography etc).

20

In the Spotlight

If you're after info contained in a specific message or email, it can take ages to scroll through a long list of messages. Access the Spotlight Search screen by swiping to the left of the Home screen. Enter a word and Spotlight will search Notes, Mail and messages.

21

Better keyboard

The iPad's touch-sensitive keyboard is easy to use. You can make the on-screen keyboard look even wider by rotating the iPad from portrait to landscape orientation. To automatically add a full stop and type the next letter as a capital, double-tap the space bar.

22

Even better keyboard

If you own a Bluetooth-enabled Apple Wireless Keyboard, go to Settings>General>Bluetooth. Turn Bluetooth on so the iPad is discoverable, then turn on the keyboard. One you've paired the iPad and keyboard by typing in a PIN code, you can tap out text using the hardware keyboard.

23

Create web clips

While you can access favourite sites by browsing through the Safari app's Bookmark folders, this can be time-consuming. To find a site more quickly, browse to it, hit the 'Add Bookmark' icon at the top of the screen and choose 'Add to Home Screen'. This creates an icon link.

24

Mail me a Note

To be automatically emailed a copy of every new note you make in the Notes app, go to Settings>Notes. Change the Default Account from 'On My iPad' to your or Gmail address. Now notes that you make on your iPad will appear in your email account.

25

Stay up to date

The latest operating systems fine-tune the way the iPad behaves, which can increase battery life. To make sure that your iPad's iOS is up to date, connect it to your computer and look in iTunes' Summary pane. Click 'Check for Updates' to discover if there's a newer version available.

26

Prolong your iPad's battery life 2

If you're out and about and need to squeeze a bit more life from the battery, you could disable Location Services. This helps various apps discover where you are so that they can find local amenities. You can turn this off in Settings>Location Services.

27

Prolong your iPad's battery life 3

Applying EQ settings (like Bass Booster) to the iPod app's songs can use extra battery power. To avoid this, go to Settings>iPod>EQ and turn it off. If you've added EQ to songs directly in iTunes, you'll need to set the EQ setting on your iPad to 'Flat'.

28

Turn off Auto Brightness

Your iPad adjusts screen brightness automatically, depending on the ambient light intensity. To manually reduce the brightness and save power go to Settings> Brightness and turn Auto Brightness off. You can then choose a less intense manual setting.

29

Charge cycle

To help prolong your battery's lifespan (the amount of times you can recharge it while maintaining 80 per cent of its original storage capacity), it is well worth charging it to full capacity then letting it drain completely once a month. Then you won't need to replace it so soon.

30

View bookmarks bar

To display your favourite sites on a bar at the top of your Safari browser, go to Settings>Safari and then ensure that the 'Always Show Bookmarks Bar' is turned on. Now, when in Safari, tap the 'Add Bookmark' icon, then change 'Bookmarks' to 'Bookmarks Bar'.

Create a more complex passcode
For a more secure passcode, go to Settings>General>Passcode Lock. Type in your current passcode and then turn off 'Simple Passcode'. Create a new code that is a mixture of numbers and letters.

Set up Restrictions
To stop your kids using the Safari or YouTube apps, go to Settings> General and tap Restrictions. Tap 'Enable Restrictions' and enter a passcode. You can then turn those apps off. You can also stop people installing apps on your iPad.

Wiser Wi-Fi
To stop your iPad automatically connecting to an unknown Wi-Fi network, go to Settings>Wi-Fi. Make sure that the 'Ask to Join Networks' option is turned on. You can also save battery life by turning Wi-Fi to Off when not using a trusted home or work network.

Back up your iPad
If you lose your iPad, you don't have to lose useful information like Calendar entries, photos and Notes. Get into the regular habit of plugging it into your computer and syncing it with iTunes to create a backup. This enables you to sync the old iPad's content with a new one.

Encrypt your backup
Another iPad user could plug their device into your computer and use iTunes' 'Restore from Backup' option to turn their iPad into a clone of yours! To prevent this, go to the iTunes' 'Summary' screen and tick the 'Encrypt iPad backup' box. It will now require a password.

Wireless sync
If you've updated to iOS 5, you will be able to take advantage of the wireless sync option. This means no more wires when you're looking to update, sync or back up your iPad, making life just that little bit easier for you. A welcome addition indeed.

Encrypt email
By default your iPad should encrypt your emails, but it's worth double-checking. Go to Settings> Mail, Contacts, Calendars. Choose an Account. Click on the email address, click on Mail then choose 'Advanced'. Go to 'Incoming Settings' and make sure that 'Use SSL' is turned on.

AutoFill
It can be a hassle having to type in a password whenever you access a site via Safari. To speed things up, go to Settings>Safari. Tap on AutoFill. You can get Safari to access personal details like your name and address by turning 'Use Contact Info' on. Turn on 'Names and Passwords' too.

Password protection
If you find it hard to remember multiple passwords, you could buy the third-party 1Password app for your iPad. This enables you to store pertinent passwords for bank, online or iTunes accounts safely and securely. It can then log you into websites with a tap.

Add more apps to your dock
By default, the dock of your iPad holds four app icons – but did you know that it can hold up to six? Just hold down on an app icon until it starts to shake and then drag it to the dock. You can also replace any of the default apps in the dock if you wish.

Quickly highlight paragraphs
There is a handy shortcut that you can use to highlight entire paragraphs without manually selecting all of the text contained within. Simply tap the text four times in quick succession and the full paragraph will be highlighted.

Quickly mute
If you need to quickly cut the sound of your iPad – perhaps to take a call or if you're someplace quiet – then all you have to do is hold down the volume down button for two seconds. Hey presto, instant silence, so you don't disturb anyone.

Create a playlist
To create a personalised music playlist, open the iPod app and click the Playlists icon. Tap Add Playlist and give it a name. Click Save. Then scroll through your Songs and tap on suitable tunes to add them to your Playlist. You can edit Playlists at a later date to fine-tune them.

Cover your tracks
If you don't want anyone to discover what Safari pages you have been accessing then you can easily cover your tracks. Go to Settings>Safari and then you will see three separate options to 'Clear History', 'Clear Cookies' and 'Clear Cache'; pick the first option.

Copy and paste text between apps

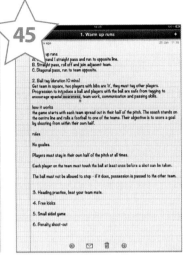

45

If you want to copy and paste text from one app to use in another then tap and hold a word (and use your finger to drag and select more text, if you need) and, once the portion of text you want has been highlighted, tap the Copy option to save it to a pasteboard.

How to delete unwanted apps

46

You can easily delete apps which you no longer use in order to free up precious storage space on your iPad. Simply press and hold on an app icon until the screen starts to shake (this is known as jiggle mode) and then tap on the 'x' next to the app's icon. You can re-download paid-for apps for free, so you'll never lose anything.

 47

Unfreeze your iPad

Sometimes you may find that your iPad's screen freezes and won't respond to touch. To get things working again, try pressing the Sleep button to make it nod off, press the same button again to wake the iPad up and slide to unlock. It should now react to touch as normal.

 48

Hard reset

If your iPad still won't unfreeze after trying the previous tip, hold the Sleep button for a few seconds, then drag the 'slide to power off' button. Turning the iPad back on should fix things. Or press the Sleep and Home buttons for ten seconds or so until the Apple logo appears.

 49

Save web images

If you find a shot via Safari that you want to keep (like a friend's Facebook photo), then simply press your finger on the photo for a few seconds and a menu will pop up. By tapping on the 'Save Image' button, you can download the shot to your iPad's Photo Library.

 50

Take a screen grab

To get useful info like flight details or train times, you often need to perform time-consuming searches via Safari or dedicated travel apps. You can then press the Sleep/Wake button and the Home button at the same time to save a screen grab to your Photo app's camera roll.

 51

Scroll up quickly

If you're reading a long document, it may take multiple finger swipes to scroll back to the top, especially if you've zoomed in for a closer look at the text. To scroll up much more quickly, simply tap at the status bar at the top of the screen. This trick works in a variety of apps.

 52

Batch-edit emails

To make your Mail inbox less cluttered, tap the Edit button at the top right. Scroll through the mails and highlight each unwanted one with a tap. A red tick will appear. You can batch-delete the highlighted mails with a click, or tap Move to send them to the Trash or Junk folders.

 53

Faster printing

Instead of syncing prints to a laptop and then printing them, you can print directly from the iPad. Browse to the shot you want to print, tap the icon in the top-right corner of the screen and choose 'Print.' You can then select an AirPrint-enabled printer and choose the number of copies you require.

 54

Subscribe to Calendars

Using the Mac that you sync your iPad to, browse to **apple.com/downloads/macosx/calendars**. Download the calendars you want and they will appear in your Mac's iCal app. Now sync your iPad (after ticking 'Sync iCal calendars' in iTunes).

55

Renaming folders

If you aren't happy with the names that your device gives to folders, you can easily rename them yourself. Just tap and hold on a folder until it starts to shake, then open it and click on the title. You can now enter whatever text you want.

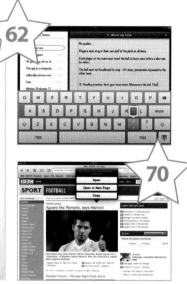

Access Google Street View in Maps

56 If you want to get a better look at a location pinned on your Maps app, tap on the circular white and orange person-shaped icon to the left of the pin's label. This will take you into Google Street View mode. Swipe the screen to take a look around, or tap the arrows to 'drive' up the street.

62

70

Lock to portrait orientation

57 The iPad's accelerometer may cause the screen to rotate when you don't want it to. To lock the screen orientation, double-tap the Home button to open the app switcher. Tap the icon at the far left so that a lock symbol appears.

Switch the switch

58 Just next to the volume controls on the side of your device is a small switch. By default, this is used to instantly mute your device but you can make it lock the screen orientation instead. Go to Settings>General and use the 'Use Side Switch to:' options.

Activating caps lock

59 When you want to tap a capital letter on your iPad keyboard, you first need to tap the left or right Shift key, which can be a hassle if you want to capitalise an entire word in your text. To turn on the Caps Lock, simply double-tap either Shift key. Tap Shift again to turn Caps Lock off.

Sync other mail

60 To sync a Google account with your iPad, go to Settings>Mail, Contacts, Calendars and tap on Microsoft Exchange. Enter your Google account details and choose to sync Google Mail, Contacts and Calendars with your iPad. For server info, type in 'm.google.com'.

Find and replace

61 As you know, you can hold down on a word in text to highlight it for editing purposes, but if you then choose Select followed by 'Replace…' you can get suggestions for similarly spelt words, which is handy way to quickly correct mistakes.

Access a secret apostrophe

62 When typing, it can be a real pain to switch to a different keyboard layout each time you need to type an apostrophe – so thankfully there is an alternative. Press and hold the '!' key and a secret apostrophe key will appear above it. Slide your finger up to type it.

Get an instant quote

Similar to the previous tip for a quicker way to type an apostrophe, it is also possible to access secret quotation marks when typing on the iPad on-screen keyboard. Simply press and hold the '?' key and a quotation mark key will appear above. Just slide your finger up to type it.

63

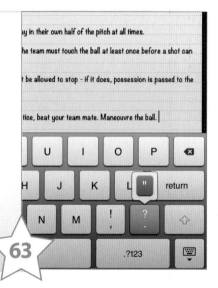

Customise Push Notifications

Many apps use the Push Notification service to send info to the iPad's screen. This can be useful or annoying, depending on the app. If you don't need to know instantly when someone has posted a comment on Facebook, go to Settings>Notifications, scroll down to Facebook and set Alerts to Off.

64

65

Turn off predictive text

The iPad's attempt to predict what you're typing can be annoying if you have to cancel wrongly predicted words. To disable this feature, go to Settings>General> Keyboard. Set 'Auto-Correction' to Off. This will also disable 'Check Spelling'.

Access websites quicker

You can save yourself a few seconds when typing web addresses into Safari. You'll have noticed there's a '.com' key to save you having to manually type it in, but if you hold it down you'll access a secret menu of other options, like '.co.uk'.

Activate Ping

Ping is Apple's social network for music lovers. By turning Ping on in the iTunes app, you can 'like' songs and share comments with friends, or follow other Ping members and discover new sounds. Once Ping is activated, you'll see new Ping icons in the iPod app's upper control pane.

Add song lyrics to your iPod app

Copy a favourite song's lyrics from the web. In iTunes, go to File>Get Info. Click on Lyrics and paste in the copied lyrics. Copy that song to your iPad. Play it in the iPod app and tap the album art in the 'Now Playing' screen to view the scrollable lyrics.

Quick rewind

When you're listening to a podcast or a talking book, you may get distracted and miss an interesting or important bit of information. Tap on the podcast or talking book's artwork to reveal the additional sound controls. Tap on the handy 30-second rewind icon for an instant replay.

Get a new web window

It is possible to open links in a new Safari window, rather than the current one. Instead of simply tapping on the link, press and hold and a new menu of options will appear that allows to you 'Open in New Page'. Slide your finger up to access it.

Control iPod sound

If you're concerned about excessive sound levels, you can limit those produced by your iPad's iPod app. Pop into Settings and tap on iPod. Tick 'Sound Check' to automatically limit the maximum level. You can set a maximum level manually using the Volume Limit option.

Create a Genius playlist

One way to find similar songs in your iPad's music library is to tap on the Genius icon in the 'Now Playing' screen's top control bar. This will create a Genus Playlist containing songs by similar artists. You can save that playlist, or Refresh it for an alternative mix.

Find words in webpages

You can search for words in Safari webpages. Type the word into the Google search box and then a list of suggestions will appear. Go to the bottom of the list to see options for 'On This Page' and then slide your finger over the Find option.

Disable email sounds

It can be annoying when you're listening to the iPod app and then the chime to signify a new email arriving interrupts the current song. You can disable the sounds of incoming emails and various other things by going to Settings>General>Sounds.

Get larger email previews

The Mail app on the iPad previews just two lines of each email by default. If you think it will be better to preview more before you tap on it (just to see if it is worth opening), go to Settings>Mail Contacts, Calendars and then tap Preview under the Mail section.

Turn off push mail

Your Mail app defaults to Push when delivering emails, so they are shoved into your inbox whenever they are sent. If you want to snatch back control over when your new emails arrive, go to Settings>Mail, Contacts, Calendars>Fetch New Data and then set your preferences.

How to delete photos

If you need to free up storage space on your device, you can delete images and screen grabs from your Photos app. To do this, tap on the Share icon in the top-right corner and then tap on the images you want to erase. When they have been selected, tap Delete.

78 **Enjoy a slideshow**
Instead of swiping through shots in a photo album, play it as a slideshow. Tap to view the first shot. Tap on the Play icon at the bottom to open Slideshow Options. Tap on Transitions and choose wipe or dissolve. Turn Play Music on and choose a track from your music library.

79 **Updating your apps**
Apps are regularly updated to eradicate bugs and add new features. To see if there are updates available for your apps, go to the App Store and tap Updates. You will then be presented with a list of possible updates, so simply tap on the Free link to download it.

80 **Watch full-screen videos**
To watch full-screen videos in the YouTube app, turn your iPad to the landscape orientation, then double-tap the video to zoom in further and get rid of those black borders. Now sit back and enjoy the videos as they are meant to be seen.

81 **Add friends in Game Center**
Game Center is great for playing against friends in online games. To add new friends, tap on the Friends category and then 'Add Friends'. You can now enter their nickname or email address to send a friend invite. Once accepted, they'll be added to your list.

82 **Get more Game Center games**
To search for games that support Game Center, launch Game Center and tap on the Games category. All your current games will be shown here; scroll to the bottom of the page and hit 'Find Game Center Games' to search for more.

83 **Play mates online**
If you want to set up an online game against friends, launch the game and then select the relevant multiplayer option. A box will now appear in which you can be matched against strangers or 'Invite Friend'. Choose this and any friends currently playing can be selected to participate.

84 **Turn your iPad into a digital photo frame**
If you want to show off your photos to friends, there are a host of options. Go to Settings>Picture Frame and you'll see a page of options that relate to your Slideshows. Here you can set the transition, the time each photo is displayed for and more.

85 **Access Flash content**
The Safari web browser doesn't support Adobe Flash. But there is an app that allows you to view Flash content on your iPad. In the App Store, search for Skyfire Browser (£2.99/$4.99). When launched, tap the Videos button in the bottom corner to scan for Flash content.

86 **Stream a podcast**
You may be accessing you favourite podcasts by downloading them to your Mac/PC and then syncing them to your iPad. To save time, use the iPad's iTunes app to browse to the Podcasts page. Tap on a podcast's title and it'll immediately start streaming to your device.

87 **Transfer purchases**
If you buy a song or app via your iPad, keep it safe by transferring it to your Mac or PC. Connect the iPad to your home computer and wait until it appears in iTunes. Now right-click on your iPad's icon in the Devices pane and choose 'Transfer Purchases'.

88 **Useful information**
It can be useful to know how much space you have left on your iPad without having to sync it to a home computer. Go to Settings>General and tap on 'About'. You can see how many songs, videos and apps you've got stored on your device, as well as any remaining space.

89 **Faster searches**
To speed up searches, you can Spotlight not to bother looking in certain places on your iPad. Go to Settings>General and tap 'Spotlight Search'. You can tap to untick specific categories. You can also drag to rearrange the order of the search result categories.

90 **Add a signature**
When you send an email from your iPad, you'll probably end it with the same signature (like 'Cheers, John Smith' for example). Get the iPad to type your signature automatically by going to Settings>Mail, Contacts, Calendars. Tap on 'Signature' and type in the text field.

91 **Add PDFs to iBooks**
If someone emails you a PDF (like your flight details), it can be tricky to read in Mail. Tap on the Share icon at the top left and choose 'Open in iBooks'. You can then access individual pages more easily, turn up the brightness and store the PDF on a bookshelf for easier access.

92 Erase all data

If you want to sell your old iPad, it makes sense to ensure that all your personal data is securely erased (though don't do this until you've backed up the device via iTunes!) Go to Settings>General and tap Reset. Then tap on 'Erase all Content and Settings'.

93 Watch live TV

There are apps to help you view retrospective TV, but what about the live stuff? In Safari, go to **ipad.tvcatchup.com**, sign up and you'll be presented with a full list of channels that you can watch for free. Tap the 'Add Bookmark' icon to add a shortcut icon to your home screen.

94 Share files

By downloading the free Dropbox app onto your iPad and setting up a Dropbox account, you can access files from the online Dropbox storage cloud via your iPad. This enables you to view images, movies and documents without needing to store them on the iPad.

95 Move apps between screens

If you want to move a downloaded app to a different screen, you'll have to do so manually. Press and hold on the icon until it shakes and then drag it to the side of the screen. After a second or two it will shift to the previous or next screen.

96 No place like home

Your iPad can have up to 11 home screens full of folders. When using an app, return to the last home screen with the Home button. Press it again and you'll quickly scroll sideways to the first (main) home screen. Press Home twice rapidly to bring up the app switcher.

97 White on black

By default the iPad displays black text on a white background. If you do a lot of reading, you may find it easier to read white text against black. To get this look, go to Settings>General>Accessibility. Turn the 'White on Black' option to On and your colours will invert.

98 Triple-click

As well as using the Home button to return to the Home screen and activate the app switcher (double click), you can assign a function to three button presses via Settings>General>Accessibility. Turn on Triple-click Home and use it to toggle accessibility functions.

99 Special characters

Some foreign words require letters that vary slightly, like Ç instead of C. To find and type foreign variants of a particular letter using the iPad's keyboard, simply press and hold your finger over the letter. New keys will appear showing the variations of that character.

100 Use the Guide

If a particular iPad feature flummoxes you, then the official iPad User Guide is a only few taps away. Go to the Safari app and click on the Bookmarks icon at the top of the screen. Tap the 'Bookmarks' link and then scroll down to the iPad User Guide.

Tips

Extend the functionality of your iPad and learn how to get the most out of the tools you have on offer

20
Browse in private

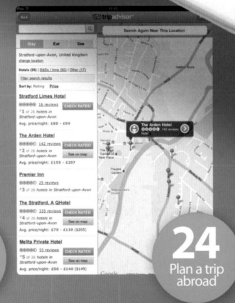

24
Plan a trip abroad

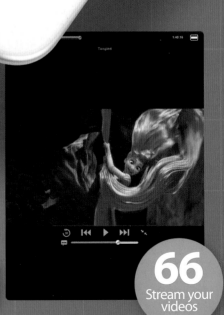

66
Stream your videos

Tips

Tips

Find out how to get more from your device and open up a world of new possibilities.

Browse the internet privately on your iPad

The iPad's web browser knows where you've been. But what if you don't want people to know which sites you've visited?

App used:
Full Screen Private Browsing

Price:
Free

Difficulty:
Beginner

Time needed:
5 minutes

Normally, when you use a web browser on your iPad or desktop computer, your movements are tracked. By default, every site you visit is recorded in the browser's history, and 'cookies' – little snippets of information – remember when and where you visited, and what you did.

There's a valid reason for this – it makes revisiting sites at a later date a lot easier – but you might not want your browsing habits exposed to the world.

Many desktop web browsers have a 'privacy' mode. In this mode, sites you visit aren't stored in the browser history, and cookies are ignored. But Safari on iOS 4 lacks that feature, so that every site you visit is recorded. You can manually clear your browser history, but that requires a diligent approach.

But there is an alternative. Full Screen Private Browsing, a free download from the App Store, is a simple, functional web browser. It lacks a 'history' function, and doesn't record cookies, so there's no way for you – or others – to retrace your steps.

Full Screen Private Browsing | Browse the web in private

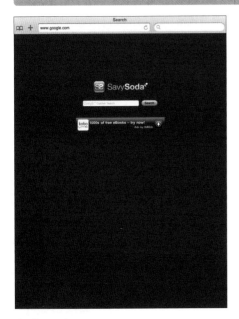

1: Opening screen
You're taken immediately to a customised Google home page. If you're searching for something, enter it in the search field.

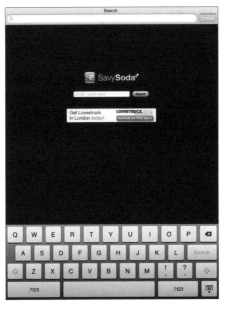

2: Visiting websites
Alternatively, enter the name of the website in the URL field. This isn't remembered by the browser – there isn't even a 'Back' button.

3: Reloading pages
The only evidence that a site is loading is the icon in the top left which spins when a site is loading. Reload a page by hitting Reload.

Browsing privately

The best parts of browsing sites in private

Google searching

The browser window always opens at a tailored Google search page, but you can also search the web at any time through this search field

Storing bookmarks

Full Screen Private Browsing doesn't share your existing Safari bookmarks, so you'll need to add your own. Unlike your history, these are stored between browsing sessions

A bigger screen

Full Screen Private Browsing doesn't just offer privacy. The lack of a bottom navigation menu means that the program's viewing area is slightly bigger than Safari's

Safari-like performance

The program uses the same underlying 'webkit' web engine as Safari, so sites should appear similar to how they do on Apple's browser

Secret Safari browsing

You can wipe your tracks in mobile Safari using a special trick. When you've finished browsing, hold down the 'Sleep/Wake' button until you see the 'Power Off' slider. Now, hold down the Home button until the Home screen appears.

4: Adding bookmarks

When you visit a site you want to bookmark, tap the '+' icon, and then the 'Add Bookmark' floating icon that appears in the middle.

5: Managing bookmarks

The site is now added to your bookmarks list. This list is permanently stored, so don't add sites that you want to keep from prying eyes.

6: Start afresh

If you quit an application and relaunch it, you'll see there's no record of your visit, as the program doesn't store browser history.

Recording...

Tap screen to stop.

Dictate notes, texts and emails

Give your fingers a rest – you can dictate notes and text to your iPad using voice recognition software. And the results are surprisingly good

App used:	Dragon Dictation
Price:	Free
Difficulty:	Beginner
Time needed:	5 minutes

The iPad's neat software keyboard has proved to be a lot more user-friendly than its detractors gave it credit for. But there are still times when you'd rather not rely on it too.

Wouldn't it be good to treat your iPad as your virtual assistant, and dictate messages to it? The good news that you can. A free voice recognition app, Dragon Dictation, converts your spoken words into text. The results can be exported to the iPad's Mail app, or shared with any other iPad app.

If you're thinking that such a small app might not produce reliable results, you'd be surprised. Dragon Dictation's voice recognition software really is impressive. This is mainly because translation is done remotely: you speak into the app, and from there it's transmitted to the developer's servers, where it is translated and sent back to your iPad. That sounds like a roundabout approach, but it's surprisingly fast and accurate. Here's how to get the most out of spoken text on your iPad...

Dragon Dictation | Dictate on the iPad

1: Set up language and settings
You'll first have to set up your language and other settings. Dragon can import your contacts list for easier recognition.

2: Tap to record
Tap the button to record, and speak clearly into the microphone naturally for anything up to 30 seconds. The red bars indicate your voice level.

3: Analysing your voice
When complete, click the 'Done' button, and in a second or two the words you've spoken should appear on the editing screen.

Using voice recognition

Get recording with no hassle whatsoever

◯ Keep recording

Tap the button to start another voice recognition session. The program can handle up to 30 seconds of text, but you'll get quicker results if you use shorter time periods

Adding punctuation

Dragon Dictation can understand more than words. If you say, 'full stop', 'question mark', or 'new paragraph', for example, the app will understand the context and add the appropriate punctuation to your text.

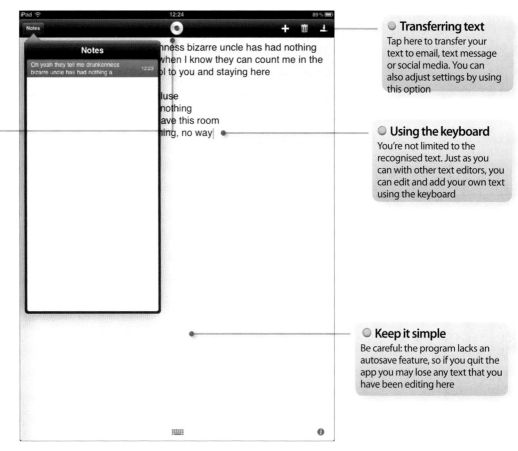

◯ Transferring text

Tap here to transfer your text to email, text message or social media. You can also adjust settings by using this option

◯ Using the keyboard

You're not limited to the recognised text. Just as you can with other text editors, you can edit and add your own text using the keyboard

◯ Keep it simple

Be careful: the program lacks an autosave feature, so if you quit the app you may lose any text that you have been editing here

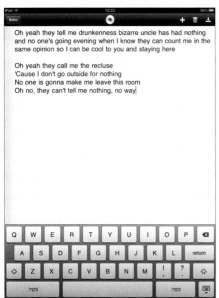

4: Correcting errors

You can edit text by clicking the keyboard button on the left, and add or remove text, or even paste text via the iPad's clipboard.

5: Export the results

Tap the button in the top right to open up your export options: SMS messaging, email, or the web versions of Facebook and Twitter.

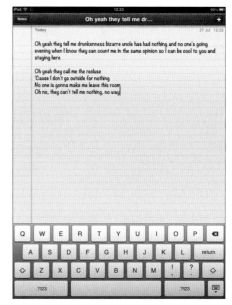

6: Copy and paste

The results are open to just about any app. Tap the Copy button, launch the relevant app, place the cursor in position, and double tap.

Plan a trip using your iPad

Looking to get away from it all? With your iPad in hand, you can find the best getaways at the keenest prices

App used:
TripAdvisor

Price:
Free

Difficulty:
Beginner

Time needed:
20 minutes

As little as 20 years ago, most of us planned our holidays with a high street travel agent. But access to cheap flights and the ability to book directly has allowed us to take control of our own travel arrangements.

The TripAdvisor website (www.tripadvisor.com) has earned a good reputation as a reliable service for travellers, particularly as it features unbiased reviews and suggestions submitted by fellow travellers. Add to this mix the iPad, which has made a name for itself as a useful travel companion in its own right.

TripAdvisor brings the website with you wherever you go. You can search for hotels, restaurants and other attractions, and it will even find flights for you. It also offers access to online forums, where other users offer advice and recommendations.

The app adds power of its own, as it's truly mobile and offers location awareness. That combination can revolutionise the way we travel. In practice, it can interrogate TripAdvisor to find good hotels or restaurants.

TripAdvisor | Plan a perfect break

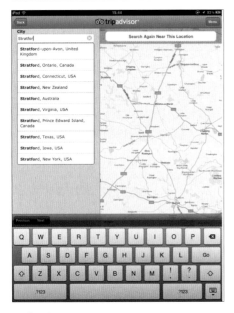

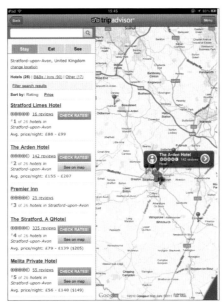

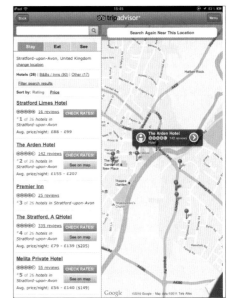

1: A place to stay
Tap the 'Hotels' link, and enter the address to which you're travelling. TripAdvisor offers a list of suggestions. Tap one, then hit 'Find Hotels'.

2: Cheapest and the best
TripAdvisor divides results into hotels and cheaper guest houses, ordered by price or rating, with a link to book a room.

3: Booking the hotel
Tap 'See on Map' to see where your chosen hotel is, and 'Check Rates' to see price availability for the dates you're interested in.

TripAdvisor travel tips

Getting the most out of TripAdvisor

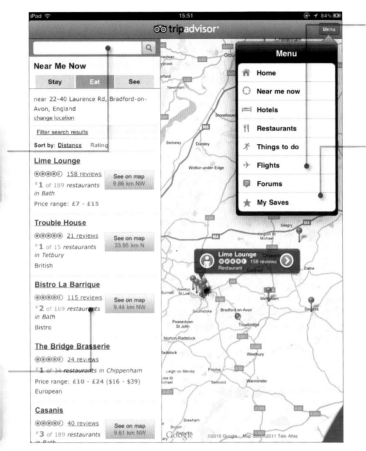

● General information

Want general information about a destination? Enter its name here, tap the Search icon, and TripAdvisor will mine its database for everything about it

● Travellers' tales

For general research about your trip, visit the TripAdvisor forums. This area offers non-specific advice, tips and chat organised by the region or topic

● Flight control

You can even search for cheap holiday flights. Tap here, enter your travel details, and TripAdvisor will search its travel partners for available flights

● My Saves

It's easy to pick up great travel titbits. If you click the Save button on any page, the results will be stored, and can be opened here

What's the catch?

TripAdvisor is a great free resource – so how does it make money? In two ways: from on-site adverts, as well as through affiliate agencies, such as airlines and hotel booking services, which supply results when you search TripAdvisor.

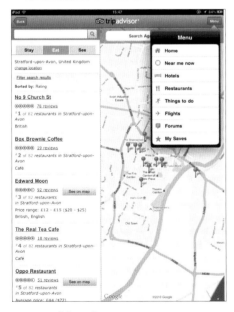

4: Good local restaurants

On the Home screen, tap 'Restaurants'. Check the 'Find restaurants near me now' option, and filter by the type of cuisine and price.

5: Things to do

Tap 'Things to do', choose to find attractions that are near you, and then pick the type of attraction you wish to visit.

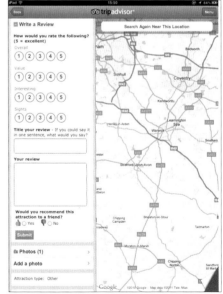

6: Speak your mind

Tap 'Write a Review', and enter the name of the hotel, restaurant or activity. Click 'Submit' to add your review.

Make calls using FaceTime

It's one of the most exciting features of the iPad 2, the ability to make video calls. Here's how you sign up and then call someone for a video conversation

Difficulty: Beginner **Time needed:** 10 minutes

The addition of dual cameras to the iPad 2 was one of the worst kept secrets yet most anticipated features of the device's launch. Not so much for the ability to go out and take pictures with your iPad, but for video calling and video capture and transmission.

Yes, FaceTime arrived on the iPad 2 and it had its very own app. If you're used to an iPhone where FaceTime is built in to the phone app then this is slightly different. The cameras are the same resolution, so if you think your main screen image looks soft, it's because it's being displayed at the huge iPad size, not a tiny iPod touch screen size.

The first thing you need to have in place before any calls are made is to register FaceTime using your Apple ID. This is the ID that is used by Apple and the App Store for purchases. Once the Apple ID is set up for the FaceTime account then an email address needs to be assigned to it. This is the one that you will use to call other people and that they will use to call you.

FaceTime | Register FaceTime and make calls

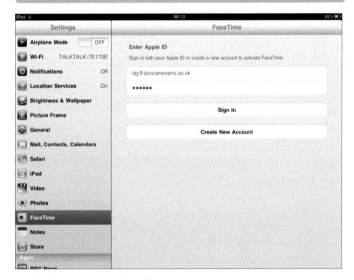
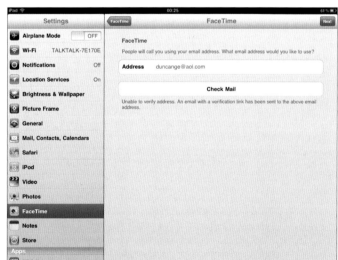

1: Register your details
Tap on the Settings app and scroll down the list of built-in apps until you get to FaceTime. Tap on this and toggle FaceTime On. You will need to enter your Apple ID. Enter the email and password and tap on Sign In.

2: Select an address
FaceTime can use different email addresses. Enter which one you want to use for calls. If it's the same as your Apple ID account it will be verified immediately. If it's different it will send a verification link to that address.

Making a call

It's easy to make FaceTime calls. Just find your contacts who actually use it and call away

○ Cameras in use
When activating FaceTime for a call, the first thing you see is yourself. When FaceTime connects the call, this window shrinks to a postage size so you can still see yourself and this main window fills with the video from the contact

○ Making contact
The names in this list aren't ones you've logged as FaceTime users, it's everyone in your Contacts database. Tap on a name to see if they have a FaceTime email you can use

Dual cameras
The real advantage of having front and rear-facing cameras in a FaceTime call is that either the person calling or the one receiving, or both, can turn the other camera on and show the other person something that is going on in front of them. All you need to do is tap the camera symbol with the rotating arms to switch your camera from front facing to rear facing.

○ People in touch
The list of Recent calls covers both those ringing you and you ringing them. If it's a frequent contact you want to call, it's quicker to tap here than scroll through the entire contacts list for someone's details

3: Get into FaceTime
Once verified, your details will be displayed and FaceTime will be on. Exit Settings and tap on the FaceTime app. This shows the display from the front-facing camera. Tap on the Contacts box at the bottom to list them.

4: Make a call
Tap on the person to call. If they have a FaceTime account the email address will be shown with a blue video camera next to it. Tap on the email address to make the call. This will then ring the contact.

Take photos with Photo Booth

Photo Booth is capable of applying weird and wonderful camera effects and using both the front and rear-facing cameras on your iPad 2. It's a bit crazy, but also tremendous fun…

Difficulty: Beginner **Time needed:** 5 minutes

Photo Booth made its debut on the Mac some years ago, when built-in iSight cameras became standard across most models of Apple computers. Now thanks to the cameras on the iPad 2, it has made its way to the device and it's a fun way to take snapshots of yourself and your friends, or just to take strange-looking photos of anything you can point a camera at.

The app itself is a little more limited on the iPad for some reason, with fewer effects and without the ability to record video with effects, but it's still great fun to play with. The touch screen interface means that when effects have a focus point, which is to say that they distort the image based on a certain area of the screen, you can use your finger to change the position and so edit the effect. Some of the others are just on or off – they can't be edited. Of course you are also able to use either the front or rear-facing cameras depending on whether you wish to photograph yourself or someone else.

Photo Booth | Take pictures in Photo Booth

1: Fire it up
Open Photo Booth and it should default to using the front-facing camera. You'll see a range of different crazy effects and if you tap on one, you will get to see that effect in full screen.

2: Light Tunnel
This is the Light Tunnel effect and if you drag with your finger, you will be able to position the centre of the effect over any part of the screen. This applies to other effects that distort the image.

Using Photo Booth

Use Photo Booth's wacky effects to create fun and outlandish pictures to share or use on social networking sites…

The image

The weird and wonderful results of Photo Booth's effects can be seen on the main screen. This is a thermographic effect

Take a picture

Press the shutter button to take a snapshot and the image will be saved to a special camera roll inside Photo Booth. Form there, pictures can be deleted, viewed or emailed

Effects

To return to the effects list, click the effects icon. You will be able to choose from the built-in effects such as pinch, twirl, X-ray, mirror and a host of other strange ones

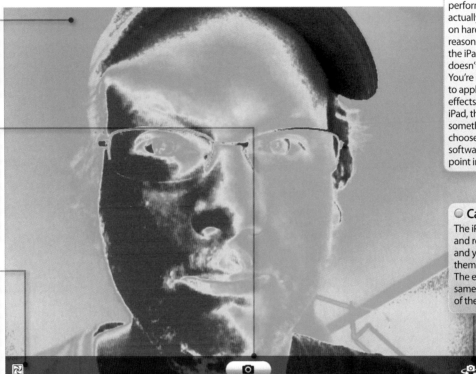

Hardware requirements

The kinds of real-time image processing performed by Photo Booth actually place quite a strain on hardware, though the reason it isn't included on the iPad 1 is because it doesn't have any cameras. You're not able at present to apply Photo Booth effects to video on the iPad, though this may be something that Apple chooses to unlock with a software update at some point in the future.

Camera flip

The iPad 2 has both front and rear-facing cameras and you can flip between them by using this icon. The effects all work the same way through both of the cameras

3: View your pictures

Pictures that you take are shown along the bottom. Scroll around and load up any one to view it full screen. Click the camera chooser to flip to the rear camera, or the effect icon to choose a different effect.

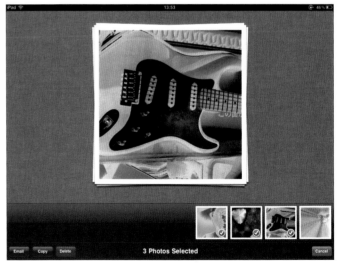

4: Share pictures

Click on the Share button and you can choose a number of pictures to either place in an email, copy, or delete. They are shown in a helpful stack view. If you deselect a picture it 'slides' out of the stack.

Capture passport-style photos on your iPad

You may think it's easy to take passport-style photos on an iPad, and it is. Additionally, experience the atmosphere of the photo shoot

App used:
IncrediBooth

Price:
£0.69/$0.99

Difficulty:
Beginner

Time needed:
5 minutes

In a world dominated by digital cameras and smartphones, it is likely that you have not visited a photo booth in quite a long time. Indeed, the only time most people visit one is to get a passport photo taken when their current one has run out. There is, however, a way to relive the good old days of the photo booth with your iPad, and it is called IncrediBooth.

When you consider that the photo booth could bring personality and life to romantic moments, and even the mundane passport photo moment, it is far from a bad thing to experience it wherever you are and whenever you want. It isn't merely a novelty, though, because there are some practical uses for it. Besides capturing special moments, you could use it for documentary purposes, although we would advise checking the rules for submitting photos. We will show you how to get the most from IncrediBooth, and to relive those days when the wait for the photos to drop into the bin was genuinely exciting.

IncrediBooth | Mobile passport photo creation

1: So familiar
You will be presented with a familiar interface that looks like the interior of a photo booth. Notice the eye level guide next to the screen.

2: Take the picture
To take your first picture, point the iPad at your face, and line up your eyes with the eye level. The app uses the front camera on an iPad 2.

3: The delay
Tap the red button, and you will see the screen flicker interspersed with a flashing red light. It does this four times.

A beautiful interface

How does IncrediBooth actually work?

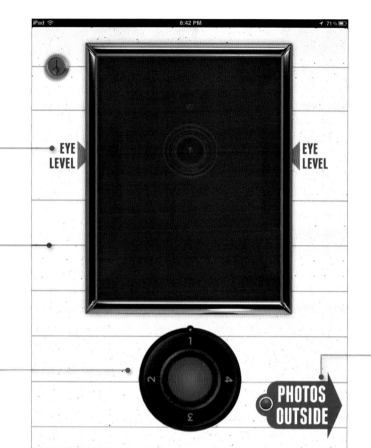

● The right level
Lining up your eyes with the 'Eye Level' line makes for much clearer photos, no matter how silly a face you pull while they are being taken

● The main screen
The main screen looks and works exactly like they used to in old photo booths. It is an unnerving experience

● Modes
The filters let you experiment a little with the colours and shading of each photo. Despite technically reducing clarity, they can add lots of personality

● The result
The way the results are presented is perfect for the mood the app creates, and the photos themselves have many potential uses once they are shared or saved

Impressive roots
The developer of IncrediBooth also makes the near legendary Hipstamatic, so it has an impressive pedigree. Many techniques from Hipstamatic have been re-used in this app to good effect, and the results are accurate representations of photo styles from years gone by.

4: Developments
Tap the 'Photos Outside' icon, and you will be presented with a film strip showing four photos. It looks exactly like an old-fashioned film strip.

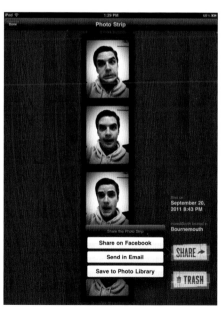

5: Sharing
Upon tapping the photo strip, you are given the opportunity to share the photos via Facebook or email. The results are impressive.

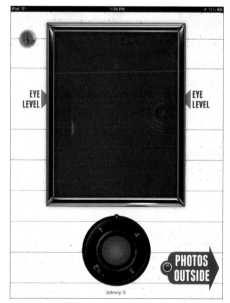

6: Retro goodness
Move the circular slider around the red button to change the mode the photos are taken in. Each uses a different film style.

Correct and edit images on your iPad

Photogene is a photo correction tool that helps you crop images, rotate them, adjust colours, apply effects, use filters and manipulate photos

App used: Photogene **Price:** £1.99/$1.99

Difficulty: Beginner **Time needed:** 45 minutes

Not every photograph looks perfect after you press the shutter button. With Photogene, you can correct an image by adjusting the colours and tweaking the exposure. You can also crop images to select just the best portion and add a border that looks like a picture frame. Thankfully, all of these tools are readily accessible on the iPad and provide a great deal of professional-level control. The effects and filters in Photogene are quite amazing. There are options to give images a cool Twenties retro look with lens shading, a black and white image, and a vivid colour treatment. Filters enhance an image with a pencil look or a posterised flat-colour look.

Not only is Photogene a good image editor, but it also helps you adjust the pixel resolution of images. For example, you can downgrade a hi-res photo to just 320 pixels in width to make it easier to email. The app also lets you post images to Twitter and Facebook, or send the final photograph via email.

Photogene | Fix your photo mistakes

1: Obtain an image
Either take a photo with the iPad 2's camera, or for the iPad 1 you can email photos to yourself and then save them to the Photo album, or download them from the web. When you start Photogene, select Photo Albums to find saved images.

2: Make simple adjustments
Before applying any filters and effects, you can crop an image by selecting only the portion you want. Press the Scissors icon (lower-left) and select the portion you want, then press Crop. Use the Rotate icon (second from left) to rotate the image.

Adjust and fix images on the iPad

Use the Photogene app to improve your images

◯ Upload
Icons for returning to the gallery, uploading to Facebook and Twitter, changing resolution, and going through a tutorial to help you get more out of the program

Add a frame
Adding a frame to a picture (icon in the lower-right) will add a frilly design or repeating pattern to the outer edge of your image. This frame is added to the outside and increases the pixel size of the image. When you save the image, the frame is also added so that, if you post the image to Facebook or Twitter, your friends will see the frame as part of the image (it is not just added to Photogene).

◯ Undo options
You can undo previous photo effects and corrections, or redo the last correction. The third icon (upper-left) allows you to return to the original image and start over

◯ Size and rotation
Photogene lets you adjust the cropping of an image to select the portion you want. You can also rotate an image left or right, and flip horizontally or vertically

◯ Effects and filters
Using the Effects button, you can apply effects such as Bleach (which removes harsh colours) or Reflect (which adds a reflection to the image). Filters also add pizzazz

3: Apply effects and filters
The main purpose of Photogene is to adjust the colours of an image and apply effects and filters. Use the Effects icon (third from left) and the Filters icon (fourth from left). To adjust colours, press the colour icon on the bottom row.

4: Upload your image
You can also adjust the colour level (the icon looks like a bar graph) and add frames and borders. When you're done, press the globe icon (upper-right) to upload your photo to Twitter or Facebook. You can also copy it to the clipboard or email the image.

Tag a photo you've taken on your iPad

Discover where your images were snapped with Location Services

Difficulty:
Beginner

Time needed:
5 minutes

There is no easier way to track the advancement of technology in the last 20 years than through cameras. Taking images and viewing them used to involve a trip to the chemists to get your camera roll developed, then waiting for a day or more while they were developed and returned – and even then half would turn out to be rubbish. Now, cameras are more accessible, as you can snap, edit and sort out images on the device itself within seconds of capturing your images. What's more, with your iPad's Camera app you can get instant records of where each photo was taken by ensuring that the Location Services are activated.

Once you've turned on the Location Services, any snaps you take will be marked as pins on Google Maps. The only downside is that there is no way to add descriptive text to the images themselves. However, there are plenty of free apps available that will allow you to do just that – just go to the App Store and enter a search for key words like 'Photo' or 'Tag' and you should find a variety of apps to suit your needs.

Photos | View the location tags of your photographs

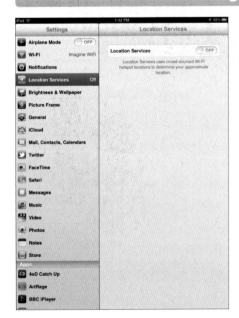

1: Activate Location Services
Tap 'Settings', and select the 'Location Services' option. If the location services on your iPad are switched off, slide the button to 'on'.

2: Switch on Camera
Underneath 'Location Services' is a list of all your apps that use Location Services. Turn the slider next to the Camera 'On'.

3: Launch Camera
Launch the Camera app, then go about snapping images. Use the Options menu to switch Gridlines on, or use the front camera.

Viewing your tags

Keep track of where your photos were taken

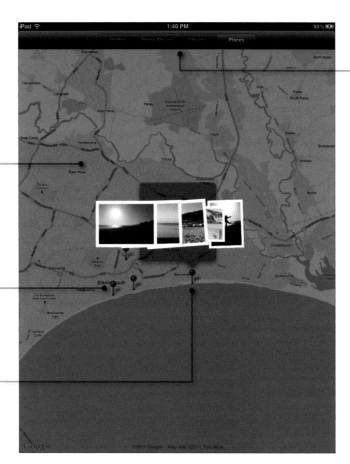

Maps
You can only view the Google Maps in 'classic' format, but you can zoom in and out by pinching the screen

Geotags
The locations of where each of your photos were taken will be marked as pins on Google Maps for easy reference

Instant access
Tap on the pins to see which photos were taken at which location, then open the photo stack to see them in detail

Switch to album
Options at the top of the page allow you to instantly switch between your photo albums and the places where they were taken

Get descriptive
Unfortunately, there is currently no way to add descriptive text to your photos using the standard Camera or Photos apps, but thankfully there are plenty of free apps available that do. Photo Name, for example, allows you to take photos and add captions in-app before sharing them with your friends.

4: Open Photos
Launch the Photos app, and you will be able to open up your camera roll to see thumbnails of all your photos.

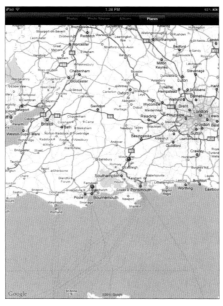

5: Go to Places
Tap on 'Places', and you will be taken to a Google Maps page with pins placed in the locations that all of your photos were captured.

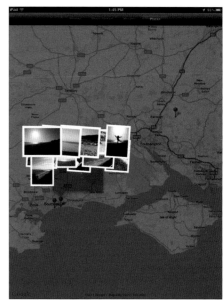

6: View tags
Pinch-to-zoom in on a particular location, and the pins will split for more accurate locations. Tap a pin to view photos taken in that location.

Keep your children entertained on your iPad

Use the fantastic Crayola ColorStudio HD app to entertain kids of all ages via an animated colouring book with sound effects

App used: Crayola ColorStudio HD **Price:** Free

Difficulty: Beginner **Time needed:** 10 minutes

 If you've got kids, it's likely that they've already fallen in love with the iPad to the point where it might be a challenge to get them away from your device. The simplicity of the tablet makes it perfect for kids, and with this new app and accessory from Crayola and Griffin, you can turn your iPad into a colouring book for a whole range of ages.

Crayola ColorStudio HD brings all the brilliance of the iPad to a colouring book app. Use the Crayola iMarker to draw on a blank sheet of paper, choose one of the pre-drawn templates to colour in, or create your own page by dragging elements onto a sheet and adding it to the 'Your Pages' section.

The best element of this app, however, is the colouring page itself. When you've chosen one, it will open, and suddenly everything on it will start to move. Each page is animated, with sound effects and music that plays in the background. Experimentation is key here, and it's great to see that developers like Crayola and Griffin are making an effort to create a fantastic colouring book application that takes advantages of all the features of the iPad in creative ways.

Your colouring book page

Complete your masterpiece

Building their talents
As your child gets older, you can change the settings in the Options menu, giving them the chance to colour inside the lines without assistance

The iMarker
The iMarker itself is a chunky plastic stylus that requires one AA battery for use, and costs $29.99. One end of the iMarker is a soft tip that allows you to paint onto the screen of the iPad, while the other is the power switch. In the middle of the iMarker is the Crayola logo, which pulses different colours as you use it.

Animation and sounds
These are automatically added to all colouring pages, giving pictures extra life. Here, for example, the ball lands in the boy's hand, and a firework goes off behind him

Filling space
If you don't want to colour-in a large space manually, you can use this Fill command to quickly shade an entire section instantly

Inside the lines
The app has editable settings for difficultly levels, but by default it's impossible to colour outside the lines of a shape – perfect for young artists

Tips

Crayola ColorStudio HD | Create, colour and share

1: Choose a page

To get colouring immediately, tap 'Colouring Pages', or choose 'Make a Colouring Page' to create your own.

2: Adding elements

Along the bottom of the screen you will see a series of backdrops. Drag and drop one onto the page, and watch it expand to fill the space.

3: Create a scene

Drag and drop parts of the image onto the page, and resize, rotate, alter the layer order, move or delete what you've added.

4: Save creation

When you've finished, save it. Select 'My Pages' so you can colour it in later, or add it to 'Your Gallery' to save the page in black and white.

5: Colour it in!

Characters will move on the screen, but when you start colouring them they will stop, allowing you to follow the lines more closely.

6: Colouring wheel

At the bottom of the screen is your selection wheel – here, choose the type of pen, pencil or crayon to use, then choose a colour.

7: Saving a scene

When you've finished colouring your picture, save it to your gallery. To view your image, enter the gallery and scroll through.

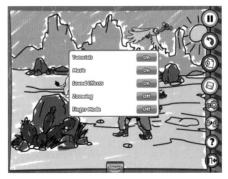

8: Finger mode

If you want to use the app without paying for the accessory, you can do so by enabling 'Finger Mode' from the Options menu.

9: Sharing is good

Choose to share your creation in a number of ways. The Email option will automatically add the image and a short explanation to an email.

Create entertaining comics on the move

Comic Life for Mac is a great way to present your holiday snaps in a different format, and now the app has made it onto iPad

App used:
Comic Life

Price:
£5.49/$7.99

Difficulty:
Intermediate

Time needed:
15 minutes

While there are plenty of photo-related apps around, we can't think of any that manage to present your photos in such an original way as Comic Life. You can add photos or sketches to a huge selection of comic templates, add text and speech bubbles, and save the whole comic. What makes it even better is the polished user interface. The app uses multi-touch brilliantly too, allowing you to zoom in and out of areas of your comic, and rotate your images or text boxes.

Creating a comic is both extremely quick and ridiculously easy. Choose a design you like and you will see an opening page. You can add photos, edit the text and move everything around, then add a new page. You have a choice of boxed templates, like classic comics, or templates that fit the design you have chosen. Each is different and each design has different effects. Playing around with this is great fun and with sharing options like emailing, adding to your Photo Library and sending to Facebook, you can impress your friends with your great comic-book designs.

Comic Life | Create your first comic

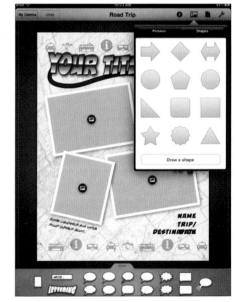

1: Templated
There are a selection of templates built into the app. You can swipe through the templates and select the one you want with a tap to have it zoom, straighten and fill the screen.

2: Basic editing
At the bottom are extra assets that you can add to your template. Drag a speech bubble or new area of text onto the page to add it, or you can use the tab to slide the tray away to the bottom.

3: Add shapes
Click the Image icon at the top of the screen to see shapes to add. There are a few basic shapes available, but you also have the option to draw your own and see it added, which is great.

4: Alternative templates

The default template is a 'Cover Page' with a large title. As you add more pages, you can choose from a selection of templates based on your theme, or more standard layouts in the rightmost tab.

5: Set up your document

Go to the Settings menu to edit the document settings. You will be taken to a blueprint-style screen where you can change the border widths or edit the comic's orientation and paper size.

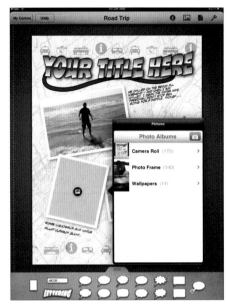

6: Add photos

Tap the Image icon at the top to browse your photo albums; or if you know where you want the picture to go, tap the icon in the frame. You can then resize, move and rotate it using multi-touch gestures.

7: Speech bubbles and zoom

You can pinch-to-zoom in on a certain area, and then add a speech bubble. You can edit the size of the bubble as well as the length and path of the tail coming out of it with a simple tap.

8: Add a page

The Document menu offers you a quick way to flick through your pages, and allows you to add new pages with the touch of a button. Touch, hold and drag to rearrange your pages.

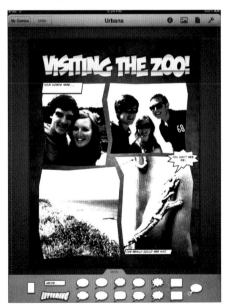

9: Change your style

Depending on the style, images will be treated differently. For example, in this black and white template, the images are given a comic-book-style effect to make them stand out even more.

Get to grips with Twitter integration

Now that Twitter is integrated into iOS 5, we show you how to instantly share your thoughts, feelings and links from within your favourite apps

Difficulty:
Beginner

Time needed:
5 minutes

There's little doubt that Twitter is a social phenomenon. This simple application allows you to share thoughts – or 'tweets' – with people around the world almost as soon as they enter your head, and likewise, see what's on the minds of people that you choose to follow.

The advent of smartphones has taken this concept to the next level by allowing you to tweet at any time, wherever you are in the world, making it easier than ever to speak your mind. Now, the tweeting process just got even easier with iOS 5.

Twitter is integrated seamlessly into Apple's new operating system; simply sign in, then begin tweeting directly from your favourite apps. You no longer need to open a specific Twitter app, find a photo to upload or copy links from your web browser; simply do it directly from within the app. It's so easy that your Twitter activity will increase dramatically once you get to grips with it. In this tutorial, we guide you through setting up Twitter integration, and how to tweet from your favourite apps.

Twitter | Tweet from within your favourite apps

1: Go to Settings
Choose Settings, then tap on the Twitter option in the left-hand column. If you don't already have Twitter installed, tap Install.

2: Log in
Enter your details – including your username and password – adjust the 'Find Me by Email' and Tweet Location options, and tap Done.

3: Tweet in Safari
Open Safari. To tweet about a page, tap the Add Bookmark option, and choose Tweet. A link to the page will be added to your tweet.

Tips

Integrating Twitter

Tweet easily from other apps

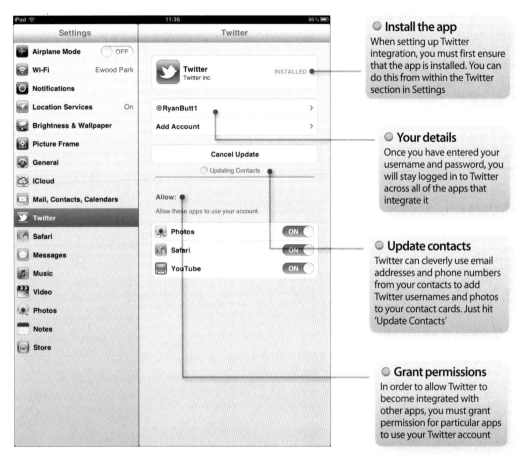

Install the app
When setting up Twitter integration, you must first ensure that the app is installed. You can do this from within the Twitter section in Settings

Your details
Once you have entered your username and password, you will stay logged in to Twitter across all of the apps that integrate it

Update contacts
Twitter can cleverly use email addresses and phone numbers from your contacts to add Twitter usernames and photos to your contact cards. Just hit 'Update Contacts'

Grant permissions
In order to allow Twitter to become integrated with other apps, you must grant permission for particular apps to use your Twitter account

Camera comments
If your iPhone 4 or iPad 2 device has iOS 5 installed, then you can also tweet from within the Camera app, allowing you to upload, comment and caption your pictures almost as soon as they are captured. Keeping others informed of your actions has never been so easy.

4: Tweet in Photos
When viewing an image, tap the share icon, and select Tweet. Any pictures you tweet about will be added as a link to your message.

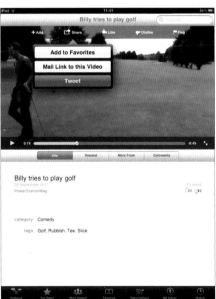

5: Tweet in YouTube
Share videos in YouTube by tapping the Share button at the top of the viewing window, then Tweet. A link will be added to your message.

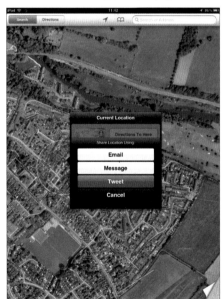

6: Tweet in Maps
Tweet your current location or places of interest by tapping on your current location, then the 'i' icon. Choose Share Location, then Tweet.

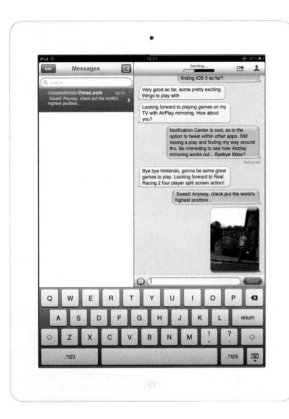

Keep in contact with friends using iMessage

Get to grips with Apple's new messaging service and send unlimited text messages to your friends

Difficulty:
Beginner

Time needed:
5 minutes

With iOS 5, it has never been easier to stay in touch with your friends and family using your Apple device. Thanks to iMessage, you can send unlimited text messages to everyone you know over Wi-Fi or 3G.

The app works exactly like the iPhone Messages app, letting you share photos, videos, locations and contacts around your social circles, and keep everyone in the loop via group messaging. To get started, simply tap the 'New Message' button, and enter the mac addresses of the people you wish to contact. Then it's simply a case of entering words into a text field, hitting the camera button to attach media, and tapping the Send button. The interface is fabulously intuitive. And it's free, so as long as the people you are contacting have iOS 5 installed, you'll be able to text without worrying about incurring a hefty bill. All of your messages can be tracked with delivery receipts (go to Settings), and thanks to the iCloud, you can also start having a conversation on one device, and finish it later on another. In this tutorial, we guide you through the process of using iMessage for the first time…

iMessage | How to text for free

1: Create a message
Tap the 'New Message' icon, and you'll be prompted to enter the mac address of the person you wish to send a message to.

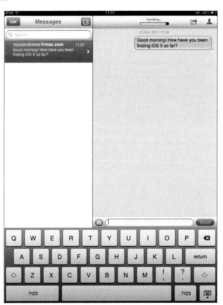

2: Type and send
Tap on the text field, and type your message into the window. When you've finished writing, hit Send, and your message will be delivered.

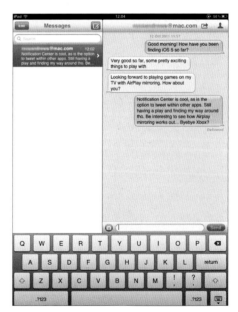

3: Quick conversations
The conversations will be neatly displayed in the main window, and the text will be colour-coded so you know who said what.

Free and easy messaging

Quickly conversing with your friends has never been so easy

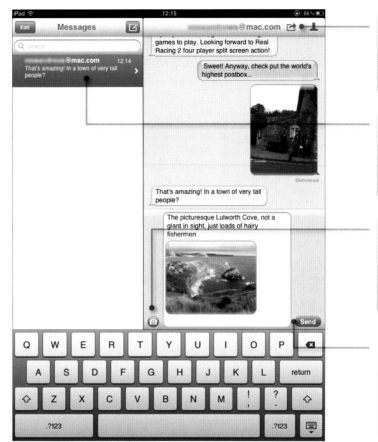

Delete messages
Delete messages by tapping the arrow icon at the top of the window and then individually selecting messages to erase

Your recipients
All of your friends will be listed in the column to the left of the window. You can bring in more people for group conversations

Adding photos
Images and videos can be added and attached to your messages. Just type your message, and then tap the camera icon to select and send media

Instant messaging
Sending messages is easy; just tap on the text field, type what you want, and hit the Send button. Each text bubble is colour-coded to make it easy to see who said what

Adding contacts
All of your Apple apps work well together. You can add contacts from iMessage to your Contacts app by tapping on the portrait icon at the top of the screen while in iMessage, and then entering the person's details into the contact page that appears.

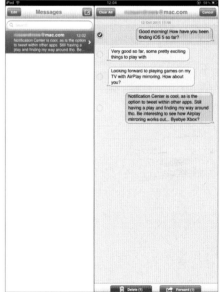

4: Adding images
Type your message, then tap the camera icon, pick a photograph from your Camera Roll, and then tap Use.

5: Notifications
iMessage works alongside your Notification Center, so if you receive any new messages you will be instantly notified.

6: Deleting messages
If there are parts of conversations you want to delete, tap the arrow in the top-right corner, and tick the circle next to the message.

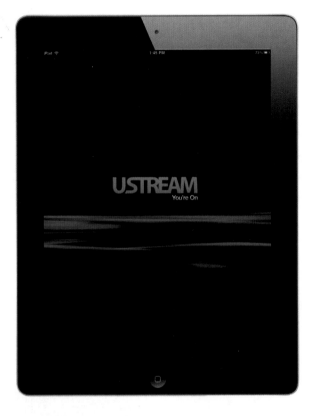

Broadcast yourself live to the world

With the help of Ustream, you can now become a roving reporter, video podcaster or anything else you want to be. It's almost too easy

App used:
Ustream

Price:
Free

Difficulty:
Beginner

Time needed:
10 minutes

The popularity of YouTube proves that millions of people want to get themselves seen on the internet, but the process of actually uploading videos could be easier. Ustream takes the idea further by allowing anyone to upload videos of themselves for others to view. Even better, you can stream your videos live.

All you need is a wireless connection and a mobile device and you're good to go, with a service that works extremely well no matter where you are. Videos can be scheduled so that people know when to start watching, which will help you gain more viewers if you make the description interesting enough.

Broadcasting live to many people is now extremely easy with an iPhone or iPad, but nothing beats the confidence of completing a few videos, which will make your creations more watchable. With some free software and a mobile device, we've reached the point where anyone can report live on events near them, and it's a lot easier than you might think.

Ustream | Broadcast on the iPad

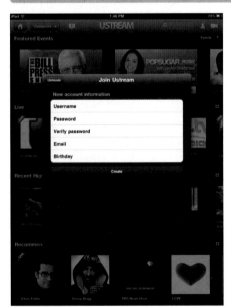

1: Get an account
Tap the User icon, and slide the Ustream slider to On. Tap the 'Sign up' button on the next screen. Fill in your personal details.

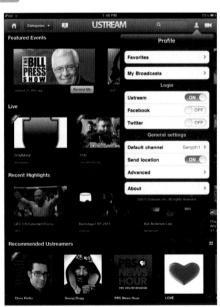

2: Check the settings
The default settings will work for most people, but it is worth checking to see if you would prefer to change some of them.

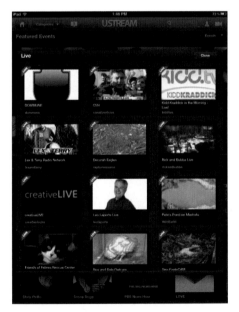

3: Familiarise yourself
You can have a look at the current live streaming videos by going back to the main screen and scrolling down to the Live section.

Live video

A look at the world of live mobile video

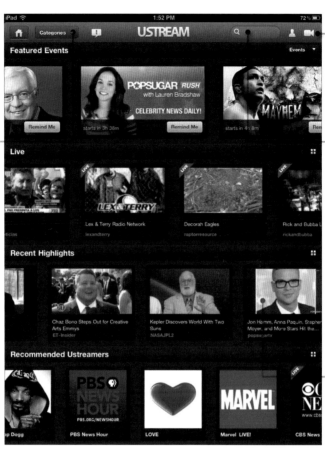

The camera icon

The camera icon is available on every screen, and simply needs a tap to start the video recording process. You can use it to broadcast live

Categories

In the top-left of the screen, you will see a drop-down menu that gives you the chance to sort the videos that are currently streaming

Unlimited content

You can search through thousands of live, upcoming and historic broadcasts, making it a viable alternative to YouTube

Gaining confidence

Don't pick up Ustream and record a live video straight away. Try to record a few to your device to gain confidence before you attempt a live stream. The more you do, the better the results will be.

True wireless broadcasting

The service works very well if you're using 3G, but Wi-Fi will guarantee a more stable and free-flowing video broadcast

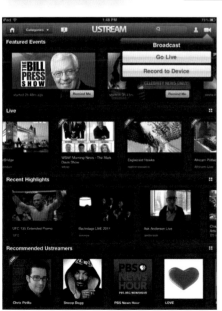

4: The serious stuff

At the top of the screen you will see a camera icon. Tap it, and you can go live, or record a video to your iPad. Choose to record first.

5: Start recording

Tap the red circle and start recording. When you've finished, tap the icon again, and you will be able to share it via Facebook or Twitter.

6: Time to share

Tap the Profile button again, and go to 'My Broadcasts'. You can upload to Ustream, and delete or share videos via Twitter and Facebook.

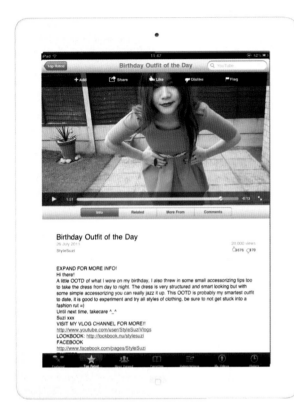

Subscribe to videos on YouTube

YouTube can be a jungle, but there are ways to tame the video giant by subscribing to content

Difficulty:
Intermediate

Time needed:
10 minutes

YouTube is one of the great successes of social media. It has launched careers, educated and entertained millions, and is great for finding and playing content.

But while there's no doubt that you can often find stunning content from literally millions of fellow YouTube users, with gigabytes of content being uploaded to the popular video service every second, it's easy to lose track of your favourite videos, or miss what might be the next big viral video.

Of course, it's possible to mark favourites, but how can you find out if a YouTube contact spots another unmissable video? YouTube offers an answer through subscriptions, which allow you to follow channels. Every member has a channel, which houses videos they have uploaded, alongside others they have added.

Once you're signed in, YouTube can subscribe to other users' channels. That means that when a new video appears in that channel, it will appear in your subscription list. Subscriptions carry over between iPad and desktop computer, so you'll always be close to your favourite videos.

YouTube | Adding subscriptions in YouTube

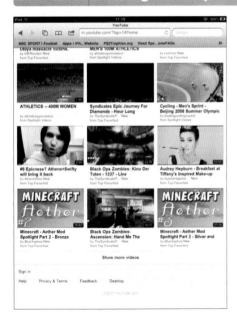

1: Signing up
In Safari, visit **www.youtube.com**. Scroll down the home page, tap Sign In, and select 'Create an Account Now'.

2: Signing in
Launch the YouTube app to sign in. Tap either Subscriptions or My Videos at the bottom of the screen, and enter your name and password.

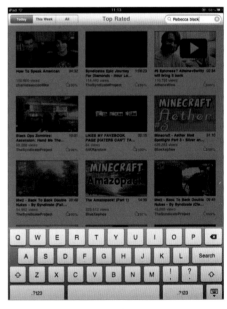

3: Begin the search
Return to the YouTube home screen, and you will see a search engine in the top-right corner. Enter text and then hit Search.

Sorting YouTube subscriptions

A look at the options of the YouTube app

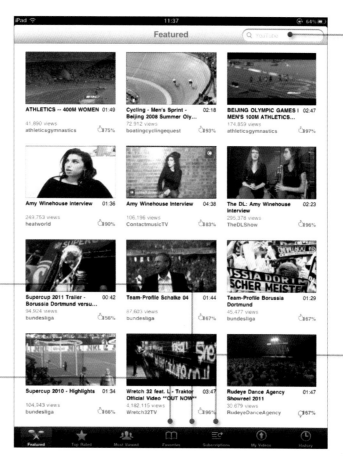

Use Search
The best way to find content is to search for it. YouTube's search engine will search titles, users and tags for the terms you enter

Promoting subscriptions
If you have a lot of subscriptions, move the Subscriptions button to the main screen. Tap the More button on the Home screen, then tap Edit, and drag the Subscriptions button to the menu bar at the bottom of the screen.

Edit menu bar
Edit the menu bar to get quick access to your subscriptions alongside your favourite videos

Favourites
Subscriptions shouldn't be confused with Favourites, which link to videos you've marked as a Favourite while signed in

Sign In
You need to be signed in to YouTube to see your subscribed videos. To do this quickly, tap on Subscriptions or My Videos, and input your details

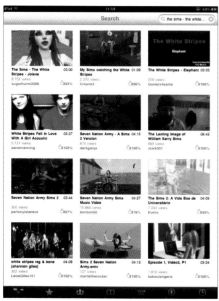

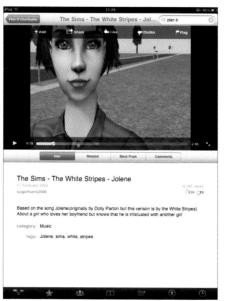

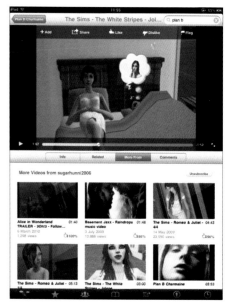

4: Homing in
It will return a list of videos. If you find one you want to subscribe to, tap on it to start playing the video and display all of the related options.

5: Getting subscribed
One of the options you'll see is 'More From'. Tap on this to see more videos uploaded from the user of the previous video.

6: Check your subscriptions
As well as videos from that particular user, a new option will appear called Subscribe. Tap this to subscribe to that user's channel.

Never miss an event with Reminders

Thanks to Apple's new task management app, you have no excuse for forgetting birthdays

Difficulty:
Beginner

Time needed:
10 minutes

We all like to think that our minds operate like unflinching super-computers. As such, we utter the doomed words, "Don't worry, I'll remember…" on an all-too regular basis, only to forget whatever it was we said we'd never forget. There is, as they say, an app for that – several hundred in fact – but now Apple has finally launched its own task management app as part of the iOS 5 update, and it's a cracker.

Reminders lets you organise your life into To Do lists, complete with due dates, notes and reminders to ensure that you never forget when something important is pressing. Simply jot down tasks, record when you need to do them by, then tick each one off as you complete it. Reminders is location-based, so if you need to pick up some groceries from the supermarket, you can be alerted as soon as you pull into the car park. The app also works with iCal, Outlook and iCloud, so any changes you make to your Reminders list will update automatically on all of your calendars.

In this tutorial, we guide you through the process of setting your own reminders and managing your To Do lists.

Reminders | Setting yourself reminders

1: Add a reminder
You can immediately start compiling a To Do list by tapping either the paper, or the '+' button in the top-right corner.

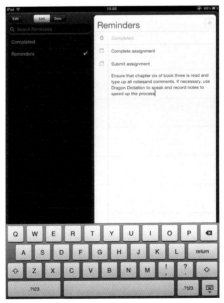

2: Make lists
Add reminders to your To Do list by tapping the page or the icon. The lines on the paper will even expand to neatly contain all of your text.

3: Add details
Tap a task to view your reminders. Tap Remind Me, slide 'On a Day' to On, then hit the date to choose when your device should alert you.

Adding reminders

Never miss anything you had planned again!

● Search
If you end up with vast lists of reminders – both new and old – then you can search for a specific reminder by entering keywords into the search window

Your system
By default, your tasks are arranged into Reminders or Completed sections. If you want to change the names of these categories or create new folders to store your reminders, tap the Edit button in the top-left corner of the screen, and then start creating new places for your filing system.

● Your reminders
Tap the page or the '+' icon to add new reminders, and they will be presented as an easy-to-manage To Do list

● Tickboxes
Once you have successfully completed a task, place a tick in the box, and it will be removed from your reminders list and added to your 'completed' list for reference

● Views
Your reminders can be viewed in a straightforward list, or on a day-to-day basis on the days you have set them for

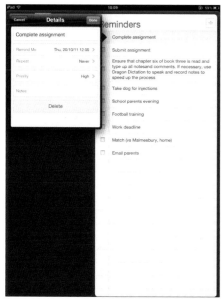

4: More options
You can set various other options, such as the priority, and add notes that relate to each task. Tap Done when you're happy.

5: View as list or date
Your reminders can be categorised by the date. To assign reminders to a specific time period, tap Date, choose which one, then add it.

6: Tick them off
Whenever a task is completed, tap the box next to it to add a tick. Reminders that have been ticked will be added to your Completed list.

Customise your Notification Center

Ensure that you never miss a thing in your work, play or social loop by setting up your own personalised Notification Center

Difficulty:
Intermediate

Time needed:
10 minutes

Your iPad has always been good at notifying you about updates, messages, events and so on. In iOS 4, however, the way in which these messages were conveyed was quite intrusive, with a message box appearing in the middle of the screen. But iOS 5 really embraces the concept of notifications, and the new and improved system features an enhanced suite to allow you to tailor all aspects of how your device communicates messages to you.

Now, you can get messages, notifications, news and the latest scores delivered to the top of your screen without disturbing what you're doing. All you have to do to set up your own personalised Notification Center is go to Settings, choose the apps, the order they appear in your Notification Center, and the manner in which they alert you. To stay in the loop, swipe down from the top of the screen, and you'll be presented with a list of notifications for all of the apps you have featured. Here, we show you how to get the most out of this great new feature.

Notification Center | How to set up and use your Notification Center

1: Go to Settings
From the Home screen, tap Settings, which is housed in your dock by default, then tap on Notifications from the list.

2: Adding items
In Settings, you can choose which apps are featured. Tap Edit, then hold the right-hand edge of each app strip, and drag it into position.

3: Tailoring notification options
Tap the arrow next to an app, and you will see options specific to that app. Choose how many items related to that app are displayed.

Setting up your Notification Center

Tailoring the news feed that is all about you

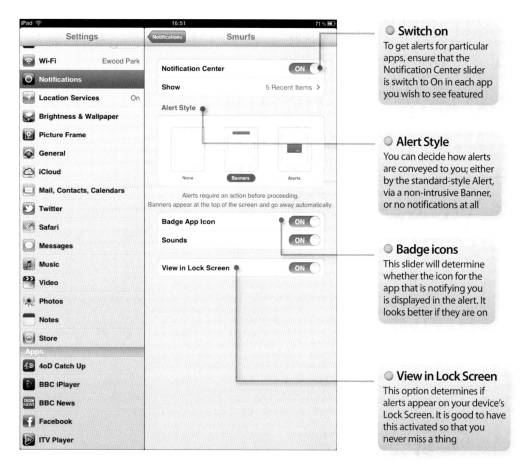

Sorting your apps

You can sort your apps on the Notification Center Settings screen by Time or Manually. Sorting by Time means that the order of alerts is based on the time they arrive. You can manually arrange the order of your Notifications by tapping Edit and then rearranging the apps by dragging them.

● Switch on
To get alerts for particular apps, ensure that the Notification Center slider is switch to On in each app you wish to see featured

● Alert Style
You can decide how alerts are conveyed to you; either by the standard-style Alert, via a non-intrusive Banner, or no notifications at all

● Badge icons
This slider will determine whether the icon for the app that is notifying you is displayed in the alert. It looks better if they are on

● View in Lock Screen
This option determines if alerts appear on your device's Lock Screen. It is good to have this activated so that you never miss a thing

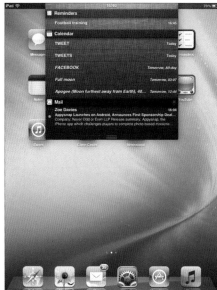

4: Accessing Notification Center
Simply swipe down from the top of the screen to call up a window of notifications based on the options you have selected.

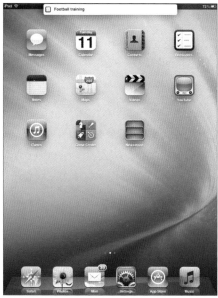

5: Your alerts
Notifications arrive in the form of a message at the top of the screen, and don't intrude with the app you are currently using.

6: Go to app
If you need to respond to a notification, tap it in your Notification Center, and you will be taken to the specific app to carry out your actions.

Sync your iCal with your iPad

It's a busy world, and you'll need to keep on top of things. Here, keep iCal and your iPad in sync

Difficulty: Beginner

Time needed: 10 minutes

The Mac's iCal application makes it easy to keep organised. It's powerful, too, supporting multiple calendars, invitations and reminders. But its real value lies in its ability to sync with your iPad to keep your whole life in sync wherever you are.

In fact, the iPad's Calendar can sync with Outlook on the PC, as well as iCal on the Mac, which can be done whenever you connect your iPad to your desktop computer using its USB cable. But who wants to be tethered? If you schedule your life using one of the calendar services offered by Apple or Google, you can synchronise your calendars between Mac and iPad over the air, with no need for a cable. This means your diary will then be up to date wherever you happen to be.

There are various options available for 'over the air' syncing, and the good news is that many of them are free. The choices include Apple's iCloud, which has recently replaced MobileMe with the recent iOS 5 update, as well as Google and Yahoo!.

Calendar | Sync your iPad calendar

1: Sync with iTunes
Connect your iPad to your Mac or PC. Launch iTunes, and under the Devices tab on the left of the iTunes window, click the iPad icon.

2: Sync your calendar
Under the Info tab, check the 'Sync iCal Calendars' box, and click Apply. This will sync iCal between the desktop and iPad.

3: Sync over the air
Go to Settings>Mail Contacts>Calendars. To set up a new account, tap 'Add Account', and follow the instructions.

Adding events in Calendar

How the iPad's Calendar app works

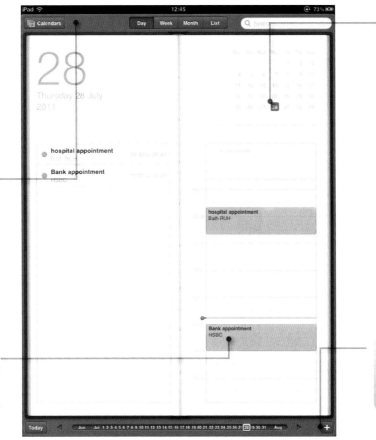

Switching calendars
Busy life? You don't need to see all your calendars at once. You can switch some of them off here

Colour-coded events
Events for the day you have selected in Calendar are listed here, colour-coded according to the calendar that they belong to

Busy days
The small black dot underneath a date indicates that there is an event or task set up for that day. Tap on the date to show the events in the list

Careful when syncing

While the ability to sync in more than one way is useful, there is a catch. If you're syncing over the air, disable syncing via iTunes under the Info tab, otherwise you may end up with duplicate calendar entries.

Adding events
Add an event to the calendar by clicking this button. The event will be synced to any other devices that you have set up

4: Turning on calendars
If you have an account, select the one you'd like to sync to, and tap Calendars to turn it on. Events you add on your iPad will be synced.

5: Limiting calendars
By default, you'll be subscribed to all calendars on that account. Tap Calendars, and deselect the calendars you don't want to see.

6: Syncing with iCloud
Open Settings, go to the iCloud settings and ensure that the Calendars slider is moved to On to sync your calendars across all devices.

Manage your finances on your iPad

Do you withdraw cash and forget where you spend it? Does your bank statement only tell half the story? Here is an app to help…

App used:
MoneyWiz for iPad

Price:
£2.99/$4.99

Difficulty:
Intermediate

Time needed:
15 minutes

As highly as we all rate our brains for retaining important information, when it comes to finances we all tend to be overcome by selective amnesia at times – usually when some spontaneous impulse buy is about to give our accounts a big hit. There are thousands of apps available to help you keep track of your finances, but few provide the depth of MoneyWiz.

Through this app, you can set up accounts for all aspects of your life – including Savings, Credit/Debit Card, Checking and Cash – input all of your incomings and outgoings, and from there track all aspects of your financial life.

A problem with other financial apps is that they're too confusing – but this couldn't be easier. As long as you have the discipline to ensure that all figures are entered and are a true representation of your finances then the app can do an incredible job of helping you track your money, stay on top of things and make savings.

MoneyWiz for iPad | Easily manage your money

1: Create an account
The app will point you towards what to press. You then need to choose the type of account, from Savings, Current, Credit and Cash.

2: Register expenses
The next step is to get used to inputting your expenses. Enter all the relevant details, and the expense will be deducted from that account.

3: Register an income
Enter all regular and spontaneous forms of income. These should include your salary, eBay sales and any other forms of income.

Keeping on top of your finances

How the app tracks your cash

● Your accounts
You can set up multiple accounts for savings, current, cash, etc, and switch between them quickly with a tap of the screen

● Your budgets
All incomings and outgoings you input are listed and categorised, making it easy to see what's coming in and going out

● Detailed reports
The options down the side of the window allow you to view your budgets, scheduled transactions and reports quickly and easily

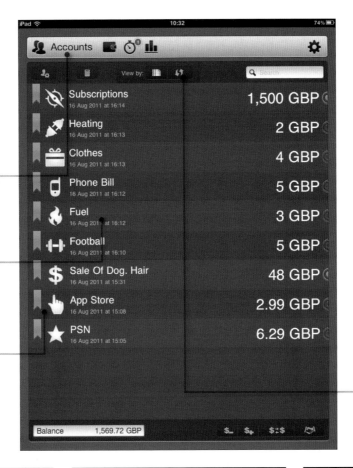

Sync everything!
Included with MoneyWiz is an option to 'Sync Everything', which is essentially an option that allows you to back up your financial data (accounts, budgets, settings, etc) on the secure, dedicated servers in the event of you changing devices. You should make a point of syncing whenever you make amendments to your accounts, so that even if you lose your device, they can be retrieved later.

● Handy tools
You can edit entries, do quick sums on a calculator and determine how your accounts are viewed, thanks to the handy top-bar options

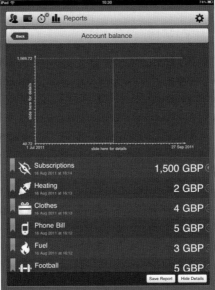

4: Schedule transactions
If you know that you have regular expenditure, input the details, and the app will make the necessary debits and credits to your account.

5: Get reports
The app can generate reports that show how much you spend and earn. These reports cover balances, an expense breakdown and income.

6: Get alerts
One of the most useful features is the option to set alerts for when your account goes into a negative balance, or your budget is getting low.

Edit and export your Keynote presentations

Keynote is a fantastic tool for creating professional-looking presentations. Here we'll show you how to get started, and then what you can do with your finished slideshow

App used: Keynote **Price:** £6.99/$9.99

Difficulty: Beginner **Time needed:** 15 minutes

Keynote makes creating attention-grabbing presentations as easy as tapping the screen and dragging a few objects around. You can choose from 12 pre-designed themes or simply create your own slides from scratch. Tap the screen to start adding text, and then import images from your Photo Album, which you can drag into position, resize, rotate and mask. You have complete freedom to create and edit your slides however you see fit, and the panel on the side of the screen lets you drag them into order.

Sharing your presentation is possible via a variety of different ways. You can email it directly from the app, copy it to your WebDAV service, or directly to your Mac or PC using iTunes File Sharing. If you're fishing for feedback, then sharing it via iWork. com works wonders. You can log into this free service (and get 1GB of free space) using your iTunes account details.

We will talk you through the basics of creating your own presentation and sharing it with others. The more you experiment, the more proficient you will get.

Keynote | **Editing and sharing your presentations**

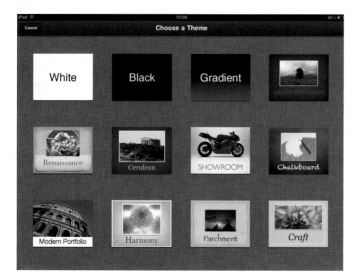

1: Create a presentation

To get started, tap the '+' in the top corner and choose 'Create Presentation'. Keynote comes pre-loaded with 12 themes to help you get started on your presentation slides. Choose one to use as a basis for your work, or simply choose a blank one and start from scratch. Then you can start adding elements.

2: Adding images

You can make your presentations more visually engaging by adding images from your Photo Album. You can import images by tapping on the picture icon on the top bar, and drag and drop to position them. Double-tap on the image in order to apply mask settings (scaling within its picture box).

Using Keynote
How to create and share your presentations

Options menu
The tool icon is the options menu that allows you access to Settings, Help and Find, plus all of the various options for sharing your work

Add some style
The 'i' icon is essentially a style icon with options tailored to whatever object you currently have highlighted, such as images or text

Animate your work
Tap on the diamond icon to apply animations to your slides, such as the transitional effects between two images

Adding images
Tap on the picture icon to add pictures. You can then press and hold to position them, and double-tap them to apply masking effects

Re-arranging your slides
All of your created slides will appear in sequence in the panel on the left. If you press and hold on a slide, then you can drag and move it up or down to re-arrange the order. You can add extra slides to your sequence by tapping on the '+' icon at the bottom of the column.

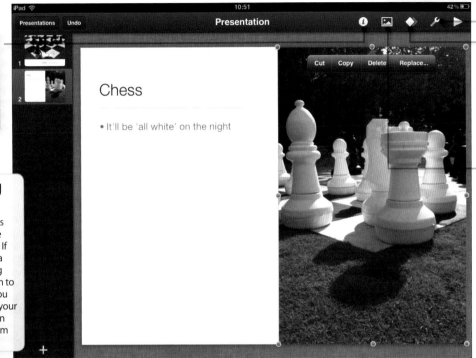

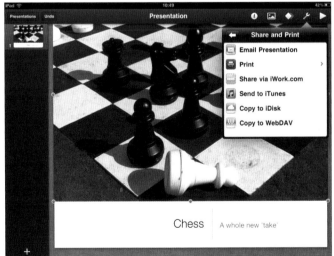

3: Adding text and animations
Text can be written straight onto the page, and then dragged into position. Tap the 'i' icon to apply style to whatever is selected (text or images). Tap the diamond icon to add animations. Try laying two shots over each other, and then tapping one to apply an animation that will determine the transition.

4: Sharing your presentations
When you have completed your presentation, tap on the tool icon on the top bar, and then choose 'Share and Print'. You will now see options to copy to iDisk or WebDAV, or share via iWork.com. If you are working on your presentations at home, then you can simply email your work back to the office.

Add images to your Pages documents

We show you how to get started with Pages and add images to your documents to make them truly stand out – and it couldn't be easier to bring some pizzazz to your creations

App used: Pages **Price:** £6.99/$9.99

Difficulty: Beginner **Time needed:** 10 minutes

Pages is an app that lets you create, edit and view documents wherever you are, requiring no previous experience of using desktop publishing packages. Choose a template from 16 pre-designed pages, or let your creativity run riot and knock up attractive documents from scratch. To finish them off perfectly though, you will need to add images, which is what we show you how to do in this tutorial.

To access your photos, you must first sync with iTunes to get them onto your iPad, or email them to your device and then save them to the Photo Album. Once placed on the page, you can also manipulate your images in a multitude of ways, such as masking. This allows you to crop out unwanted portions without editing the image itself. To do this, double-tap the image when it has been placed, and then drag the slider that appears to make it larger or smaller within the mask. You can also set the style of the picture borders, rotate, flip and layer the image, and wrap text around it by tapping the 'i' icon when the image is selected. It's so easy that you can be well on your way to creating eye-catching pages in minutes.

Pages | Adding images to Pages

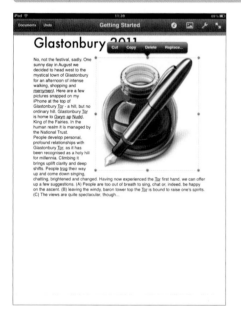

Glastonbury 2011

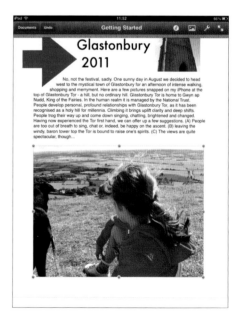

1: Drag and position picture box
Tap and hold on the image box, then drag it to where you want it to sit on the page. Once you've positioned it, drop it into position.

2: Import pictures
Tap the picture icon, and locate the image you wish to import. Images stored in your Photo Album can be found under the 'Media' header.

3: Adding more images
Tap the picture icon to select more images. Every time you select one, it will appear on the page in a new picture box.

Using Pages
Why the app is so easy to use

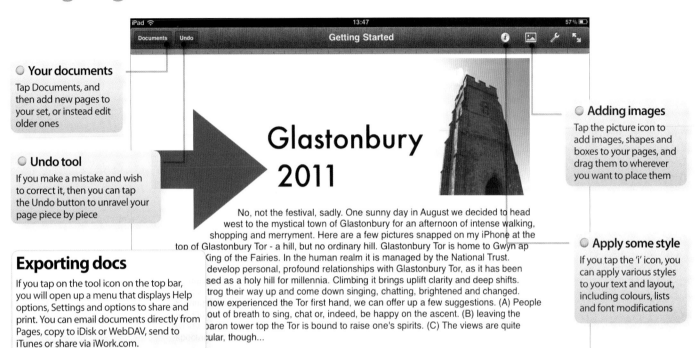

Your documents
Tap Documents, and then add new pages to your set, or instead edit older ones

Undo tool
If you make a mistake and wish to correct it, then you can tap the Undo button to unravel your page piece by piece

Adding images
Tap the picture icon to add images, shapes and boxes to your pages, and drag them to wherever you want to place them

Apply some style
If you tap the 'i' icon, you can apply various styles to your text and layout, including colours, lists and font modifications

Exporting docs
If you tap on the tool icon on the top bar, you will open up a menu that displays Help options, Settings and options to share and print. You can email documents directly from Pages, copy to iDisk or WebDAV, send to iTunes or share via iWork.com.

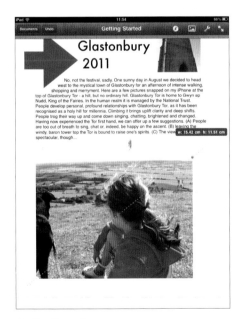

4: Scaling images
Press and hold the dots in the corners, and then drag them inwards or outwards to resize the image.

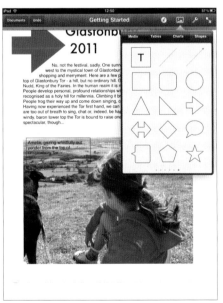

5: Adding captions
Tap the picture icon, then choose the Shapes category. To add a caption, pick the square with the 'T' in the middle and scale it accordingly.

6: Changing text colour
Tap the 'i' icon, and in the Style section, scroll to the bottom of the list and tap 'Text Options'. You can now tap on Colour to change it.

Tips

Publish Pages documents to iWork.com

Discover how you can upload your Pages documents to Apple's free cloud system and invite friends and colleagues to view and comment on them with ease

App used: Pages **Price:** £6.99/$9.99

Difficulty: Beginner **Time needed:** 10 minutes

Once you've created your documents in Pages, there are various ways to show them off. Tap on the tool icon on the top bar of Pages, and you'll bring up options to 'Share and Print', which include emailing them from within the app, sending them to iTunes and copying them to iDisk and WebDAV.

iWork.com is a web-based public beta service that allows you to share compatible files on your Mac or iPad in a way that is simple, smart and secure. You can publish your work and invite others to view it without ever leaving the apps your created the documents on – such as Pages, Numbers or Keynote.

Setting up the sharing process in Pages is easy; just tap on the tool icon, choose 'Share and Print', and 'Share via iWork.com'. After signing into your iWork account – which uses the same login details as your iTunes account – your documents will be uploaded and viewable by others within a few minutes.

The process is quick and easy and, once the documents have been uploaded, all invited parties can view them and add their own notes – ideal for when you're working remotely and need feedback.

Pages | Sharing documents via iWork.com

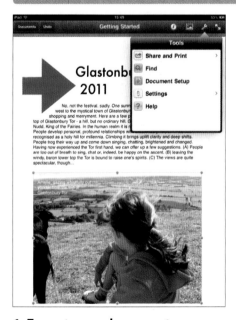

1: Export your documents
Open the document you want to export, and tap the tool icon in the top-right. This will bring up various options, including 'Share and Print'.

2: Share via iWork.com
Tap 'Share via iWork.com'. A new window will open in which you can sign into iWork.com. If you like, choose 'Create a new Apple ID'.

3: Enter details
The email and password you are required to enter are the same as your iTunes details. Once you have entered them, tap 'Sign In'.

Navigating iWork.com

How to view your Pages documents online

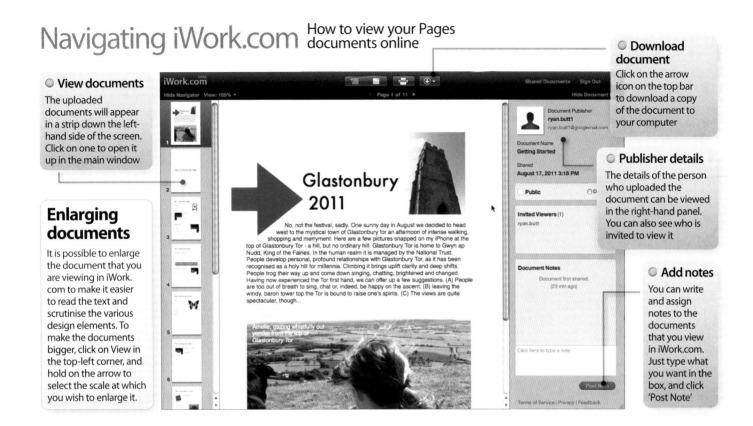

View documents

The uploaded documents will appear in a strip down the left-hand side of the screen. Click on one to open it up in the main window

Download document

Click on the arrow icon on the top bar to download a copy of the document to your computer

Publisher details

The details of the person who uploaded the document can be viewed in the right-hand panel. You can also see who is invited to view it

Enlarging documents

It is possible to enlarge the document that you are viewing in iWork. com to make it easier to read the text and scrutinise the various design elements. To make the documents bigger, click on View in the top-left corner, and hold on the arrow to select the scale at which you wish to enlarge it.

Add notes

You can write and assign notes to the documents that you view in iWork.com. Just type what you want in the box, and click 'Post Note'

4: Verify your account

The app will send you an email. When you have received it, click on the link in order to verify your account.

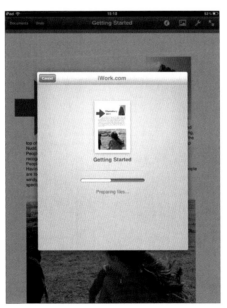

5: Upload document

Your document will begin uploading. This may take a while depending on the size. Once done, it can be viewed on the iWork.com website.

6: Viewing the document

Log in on your Mac, then click on the document in the viewing panel. You can then download it to your machine or add notes.

Tips

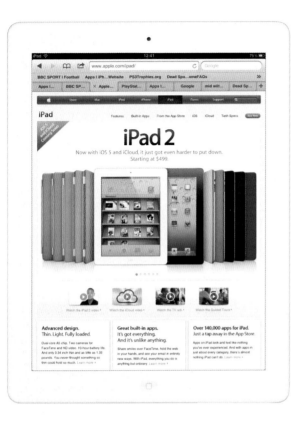

Use tabbed browsing in Safari

Discover how the already pleasurable experience of surfing the web on your device is made even easier with some great iOS 5 enhancements

Difficulty:
Beginner

Time needed:
5 minutes

Surfing the web on your Apple device has always been a simple and pleasurable experience, but iOS 5 adds some welcome tweaks to ensure that the experience is made even easier. One of the most prominent enhancements is the use of tabs to manage your open Safari webpages.

When opening new pages in iOS 4, you were briefly taken out of the main window to be presented with your pages laid out on a grid, which you tapped to call up individual pages. iOS 5 arranges all open pages in tabs at the top of the main window, allowing you to access them from the same interface. If you regularly use Safari, you'll be amazed at how it can speed up your productivity. Two other new features that have been subtly worked into Safari are Reading List and Reader. With Reading List, you can save articles to read offline, and upload them to your iCloud. Reader supplies a similarly handy service by allowing you to read articles free from on-screen clutter, such as images and adverts, so that you can be unhampered by visual distractions.

Safari | Open multiple pages using tabs

1: Launch Safari
Visit a page. If you have bookmarks stored then these will be laid out across the top of the window. Tap one to go to that particular page.

2: Open new tab
Simply tap the '+' icon in the top right-hand corner, and a new page will become available in a separate tab.

3: Adding tabs
Keep adding tabs by pressing the '+' icon to call up a new window. As more are added, the existing tabs will be pushed along the top.

Your new-look Safari window

Little enhancements that make a big difference

Reading List
Another new Safari enhancement is Reading List. If you're running short on time, add an article to your list, and you'll be able to finish it later – even on a different device

Tweet from within
With Twitter integrated in iOS 5, you can tweet from within your favourite apps without having to copy links into a separate Twitter app

Your tabs
All of the webpages that you currently have open will be displayed as tabs at the top of the screen. Tap on a tab to access it instantly

Safari Reader
To read certain articles without clutter, such as pictures or ads, tap the Reader icon in the address bar, and all non-article material will be stripped away

Cloud connect
Safari works with your own personal iCloud, meaning that any articles you add to your Reading List are synced to your iCloud and stored, so you can start reading them on an iPad, and pick them up where you left off on your iPhone later.

4: Accessing tabs
Tabs is quicker and more efficient than the format favoured by the previous iOS, as you can access any tabbed page by tapping on the tab.

5: Closing tabs
Upon reaching your limit, you will no longer be able to add new tabs without deleting existing ones. To do this, open a tab and then tap 'X'.

6: Organising your tabs
If wish to rearrange the tabs at the top of your browser window, then simply press and hold on a particular tab, and drag it left or right.

Keep updated with the news while mobile

Do want the latest news from around the globe delivered in a fun and engaging way? Then get your finger on the pulse with Flashpoint News

App used: Flashpoint News – World Pulse **Price:** Free

Difficulty: Beginner **Time needed:** 5 minutes

News apps traditionally do a fine job of thrusting the latest news stories under your nose, but lack sophistication. But with Flashpoint News, you get all the latest news from around the world tailored to your interests, and delivered in an engaging and eye-catching interface.

The app is essentially an RSS feeder. You start off by selecting all of your favourite RSS feeds, and are then presented with a world map with the biggest stories represented by dots over the applicable countries. A line then travels from country to country delivering bite-sized news nuggets upon arrival. Tap on the news box to get the full story, or jump straight to the original source to read it in full. If you can't wait for it to arrive at a destination, simply tap on a dot, and you'll be presented with a full list of stories from that particular country.

All news is updated regularly, and tickertape constantly rolls along the bottom of the screen to keep you informed. This handily mentions the country, so you can use this as a basis to jump straight there for the full low-down. It's a fun and imaginative way to present the news.

Flashpoint News – World Pulse | Put your finger on the pulse

1: Select your RSS feeds

When you launch the app, you can select your map style, and will then be invited to choose your preferred RSS feeds. If you are unsure of which feeds to choose from, then tap on Recommended. You will then be presented with a list of active feeds. Tap on the '-' icon next to each feed to disable it.

2: Get world news

If you want to find particular feeds, then you can also perform a manual search. Your chosen map will then be displayed in landscape orientation, and an *Indiana Jones*-style travel line will move from country to country, in the process providing handy bite-sized chunks of news that will flash up on each destination.

Travelling the world for news
Get the hottest stories in a fun and engaging way

Your world news
The app provides a world overview on a map style of your choosing, and a travel line moves from story to story

Options and opinion
You can change the style of the map on which your news is presented, get news on other apps from the developer, and leave constructive feedback on the app at any time simply by rotating your device to the portrait orientation. When you want to dive back into the world of news, rotate it back to landscape mode.

Your RSS feeds
The news is based on your pre-selected feeds. You can edit your list at any time by pressing the icon in the top-right corner

In the news
Each country that is in the news is highlighted on the map. Tap on it to get an instant list of stories

Tickertape
A rolling stream of news is relayed along the bottom of the screen at all times, and is regularly updated

3: Read the details
You can tap on each bite-sized portion of the news if you want to get the full story, along with any accompanying images that might be there. You can also tap on the multiple arrow icon that lies centrally in the bottom bar of each story to extend the viewing window in order to get the bigger picture.

4: Head to the source
To check out the full story from the original source, simply tap on the single arrow icon at the bottom of each story, and your web browser will divert you. To jump straight to the news from a particular area without waiting for the travel line to get there, just individually tap on the dots on each country.

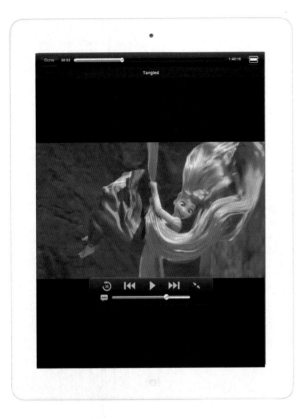

Watch movies on your iPad with Video Stream

Stream every video on your computer to your iPad, and hook it up to the TV to create the ultimate sharing solution

App used:
Video Stream

Price:
£0.69/$0.99

Difficulty:
Expert

Time needed:
10 minutes

Your iPad is fantastic for watching movies, thanks to its beautiful big screen and ability to hold huge amounts of data. However, for some users not even the biggest iPad will hold every film they have. Some may use AirPlay to access their iTunes library, but if you want a little more flexibility, there is another option: Video Stream.

Using this, you can view movies in just about any format, streamed directly from your computer. You can then convert videos within the app itself so that if you leave your local network, you can pick up right where you left off.

Video Stream also supports Video Out. If you have an Apple Digital AV Adapter or a Composite AV Adapter, you can plug your iPad straight into your TV and have your movies streamed to the big screen from your PC or Mac. Then, if you have another iPad or iPhone with the app installed, you can use the second device as a remote from the comfort of your chair. It's like an Apple TV box, but at around two per cent of the price.

Video Stream | Setting up a stream

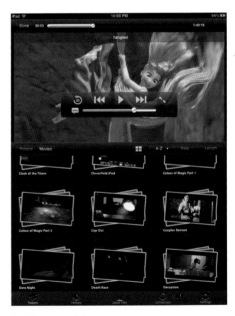

1: Connection established
When you've downloaded the server from the developer's website and opened the app, input a code to share your media.

2: Browse movies
Drag folders into the Server app to share the movies. On your iPad, you can tap the folders as they appear and scroll through the videos.

3: Play a video
Tap a movie you want to play. You will get a small preview, and tapping the full screen arrows will get rid of everything but the video.

The Video Stream interface

Navigating to and controlling a movie

● Grid or list?
Using this button, you can choose to either view the movies as a grid – like we are at the moment – or as a list to fit more onto the screen

● Tabs
Along the bottom are your tabs. Here, you can access your Folders, videos you've previously watched, local files you've converted, and any movies you're currently converting

● Speed scrubbing
You can skip through the movie quickly by dragging the bar along the top of the video. It will buffer briefly, then pick straight back up again

● Aspect ratio
In the top left is the aspect ratio controller, which allows you to fill the screen if you want. All the controls also work when connected up to the TV for ease of use

Video Stream for Mac and PC
In order to stream the videos from your computer, you'll need to download the Video Stream server for free from www.collect3.com. Downloading is quick, and sharing videos is as simple as dragging the relevant file onto the application window on your Mac or PC. From then on, you can access every sub-folder and movie within it with a tap.

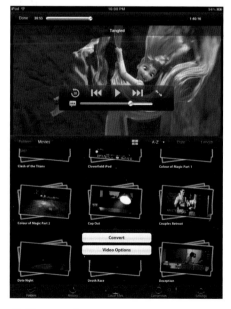

4: On the big screen
If you connect your Digital AV Adapter and plug your iPad into your TV, the movie will appear up on the big screen.

5: Remote control
When you're watching a movie on the TV, your iPad will recognise this and add a Remote tab. With this, you can control the action on-screen.

6: Conversion
If you want to watch a video when you're no longer connected to your computer, tap and hold on the file, then select Convert.

Tips

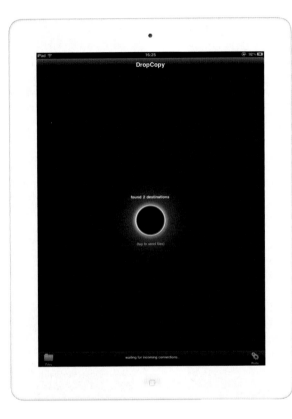

Share files wirelessly via your iPad and Mac

There are many apps available to allow you to transfer files wirelessly between devices. Here, we examine one of the simplest…

App used:
DropCopy

Price:
£2.99/$4.99

Difficulty:
Intermediate

Time needed:
10 minutes

Even a few years ago, transferring files between devices without wires, dongles and discs would have been considered witchcraft. But nowadays, there are thousands of apps available to perform this task. Apps such as Dropbox and Documents To Go are considered the market leaders, but even they require a fiddly set-up process that can take several minutes before you can start moving files between systems.

In DropCopy, we get a transferral system that ranks as by far the simplest we have encountered. To make it work, simply download the app for your iPad (a 'Lite' version that performs the task perfectly well is also available) and Mac and, provided both devices are on the same Wi-Fi network and can 'see' each other, simply drag files into the portal (which resembles a small black hole on your desktop) or choose the destination from your iPad. Text documents, PDFs, images and audio-visual content can be swapped between devices in seconds.

DropCopy | Transfer files wirelessly

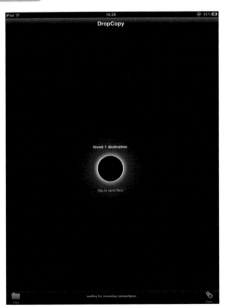

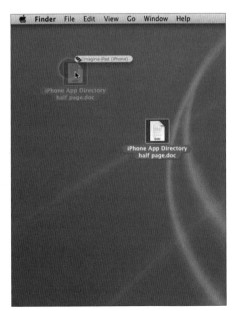

1: Download the apps
Download the app for your iPad and Mac. Go to http://10base-t.com/macintosh-software/dropcopy/ to get the desktop version.

2: Launch the apps
Open the apps on both machines. The iPad should say 'found 1 destination' to indicate that a connection has been made.

3: Transfer files
When DropCopy is launched, you will notice a circle on your desktop. Drag the files you wish to transfer into this circle and they will copy.

Your file-transferring portal

A simple app for a simple process

Destination
With the app running simultaneously on your iPad and computer, the circle in the middle of the screen shows that a connection has been established

Files
This is where all of your transferred files are stored and sorted into categories depending on the file type – docs, PDFs, images and audio/visual

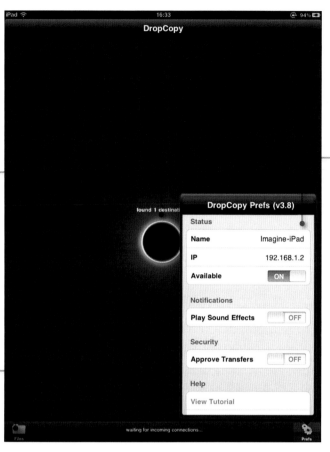

Info
The 'Info' panel provides a full tutorial for using the app, troubleshooting tips, and the option to see what additional features the paid-for app provides

Preferences
By accessing the preferences panel, you can apply additional layers of security to approve incoming file transfers and obtain assistance

Email
The most universal method of transferring files wirelessly is still emailing them as attachments, but the advantage of using specific apps to carry out this task is mainly speed-related. Attaching large files to emails can often take several minutes to send, but by using apps such as DropCopy, the process can be done in seconds.

4: Transfer complete
The files will be transferred into folders that reflect the file type. View the folder that corresponds with the file to check it's there.

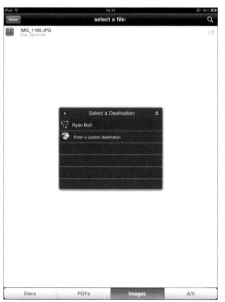

5: Transferring from iPad
Tap on the file you wish to transfer, then choose a destination. The link to your computer should be present, so tap on that to begin the process.

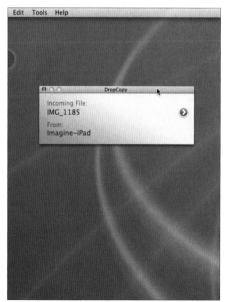

6: Message of confirmation
You will receive a message of confirmation on your computer that a file is incoming. Before too long, the file will appear on your desktop.

86 Test your eyesight

94 Create a family tree

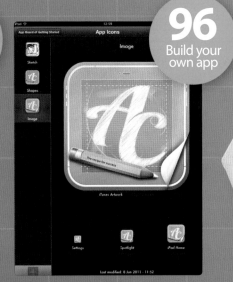

96 Build your own app

Tricks

Get creative and do things on your iPad
you would never imagine you could do

Tricks

Guides to help you power-up your
iPad and use it in ways you never
knew you could

Turn your iPad into a videogame controller

Turn your iPad into a touch-screen controller, and play your iPad games on the big screen

App used: Real Racing 2 HD **Price:** £4.99/$6.99

Difficulty: Intermediate **Time needed:** 15 minutes

The iPad is great for gaming, whether you're a seasoned player of hardcore titles like *Call Of Duty*, or someone who's never picked up a controller in their life. The touch screen and accelerometer inputs allow for all kinds of innovative but simple control systems that let you keep up with the action on the screen.

With the iPad 2, however, the functionality has increased to something beyond that of the original iPad. Now, you can invest in an Apple Digital AV Adapter (£35 from Apple's website) that allows you to connect to your HD TV using an HDMI cable.

In the day-to-day working of the iPad, this is great for things like Keynote presentations, video sharing and the displaying of photographs, because your TV will mirror exactly what is happening on your iPad screen instantly. For gaming, however, it's even better; some gaming apps have already been adapted to utilise the Digital AV Adapter, meaning you will now be able to fill your television with the fantastic graphics of your iPad 2. One of the best-looking games out there has already been adapted to take advantage of this – *Real Racing 2 HD*.

Entering a race

Getting to grips with all the information on screen

The competition
When you get closer to the car in front of you, you will see their position in the race and their name. You'll soon recognise your closest rivals

Full-screen apps
Other apps also take advantage of your full 1080p TV screen, including YouTube, Keynote, Chopper 2, and Safari, but games like *RAGE HD* have been specifically adapted for the dual screen set-up to create different displays for each screen. Other apps will mirror your display in the iPad's native display resolution, so searching for the ones that support 1080p HD is well worth it.

Assistance?
You can choose a difficulty level, which will remove the assists that are on by default. You can change them in the settings screen, too

Widescreen
You may have to fiddle with some settings on your TV, but for most users plugging in the adapter and opening the game will change the viewing mode

Graphical power
The iPad 2 really excels when it comes to graphics. When you connect it to the TV, you could quite easily mistake it for a console game

Real Racing 2 HD | Connect up and play

1: Connect her up
Plug the HDMI cable into the Adapter, and slot that into the iPad 2. You can also charge your iPad while you play if your battery is low.

2: Choose a car
There are a surprisingly high number of cars in *Real Racing 2*; each one is based on a real car, with nine manufacturers providing the licences.

3: Admire in 3D
Swiping and pinching on the iPad screen will rotate the camera, and allow you to view the car's 3D design from any angle.

4: Start your career
The Career Mode in *Real Racing 2 HD* is absolutely huge. Start a career, and enter your first race to get straight onto the track.

5: Get racing
Before each race, you will have a brief video introduction to showcase the graphical power of the iPad 2.

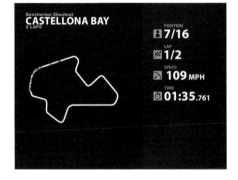

6: Map it out
During the race, your iPad displays all the information you'll need. You can see a map of competitors, as well as speed and positioning.

7: Hairpin
Thanks to the iPad's controls, turning a corner is as easy as tilting the iPad itself. The screen will tip slightly so you know when to stop.

8: Ouch!
There are two viewpoints for the cars in the game – the driver's POV, or this more traditional gaming view.

9: Result
At the end, turn your attention back to the iPad to see the results. Tap 'View Replay', and it will play on your TV while you see how you fared.

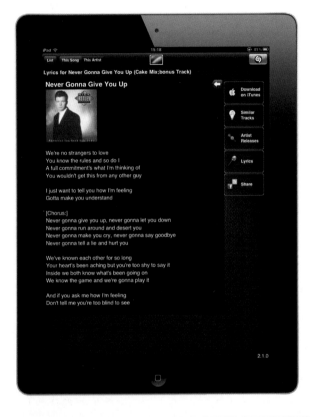

Identify and purchase a song in an instant

Music recognition services save frustration by making it simple to accurately identify songs just by listening to them

App used:	Shazam for iPad
Price:	Free
Difficulty:	Beginner
Time needed:	5 minutes

Remember the frustration you felt when you heard a snippet of a track on the radio, but the disc jockey didn't tell you what it was?

A free music recognition app like Shazam for the iPad brings that frustration to an end. It does something that we do far too infrequently: recognises music by listening to it. With a few seconds of analysis, it will 'tag' the track, identifying its title and artist. It then goes even further, with one-click access to song lyrics, so you can sing along to your new discovery, and even buy and download the song through a link to iTunes.

The free version of Shazam lets you tag up to five songs every month. That should be enough for most occasional listeners, but a paid-for version offers unlimited tagging and other features, including recommendation.

Shazam's complex recognition algorithms means that it will only identify studio-recorded music tracks. If you try to hum your favourite track, it will come up empty-handed.

Shazam | How to recognise a song with Shazam

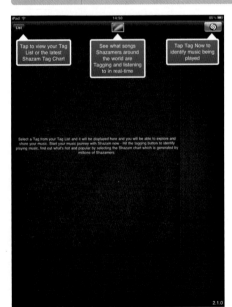

1: Get tagging quickly
Shazam is built for speed: its opening screen is a basic affair. Hold the iPad's microphone to the source of the music, and touch the large icon.

2: Analysis stage
The sound you've recorded is sent to the Shazam servers and analysed. It only take a few seconds for Shazam to return a result.

3: Showing the details
If it's successful in its recognition attempt, then Shazam will display the song's title, artist, and often a thumbnail image of the cover.

Organising music

Keeping on top of your tracks in Shazam

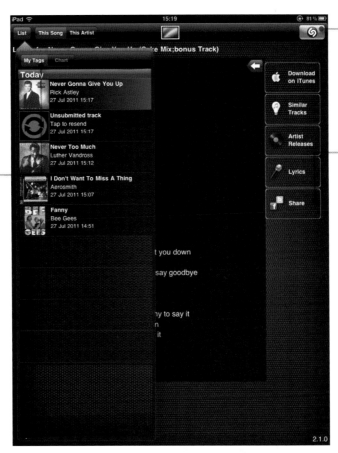

Changing settings
Customise Shazam to enable tagging when the app launches. This saves vital seconds if you need to identify a song quickly

Quick tagging
You're never far away from instant recognition: tap the Tagging button to start listening to music

Sign up
The free version of Shazam is limited by the number of songs it can tag during a month. The commercial version is free from such restrictions

Shared music
What are your friends listening to? Set up an account – you can do it through Facebook – to share the music you are listening to and tagging

Organisation is the key
If you have amassed a lot of tags then things can get a bit cluttered on the tags page. But you can organise your finds. Tap the 'i' button at the top of the screen to organise your tags by date or artist.

4: Read about the artist
Tap on the 'This Artist' button at the top of the page, and you'll be able to read a detailed bio on the tagged artist.

5: Get a full discography
If you tap the 'Artist Releases' button, you will get the complete history of your tagged artist. Tap on a song to get more options.

6: Buy the track
Tap the iTunes button to download the track from iTunes. Within seconds of hearing it, it's now in your iTunes library, and yours to keep.

Utilise settings in GarageBand to record a track

Recording in GarageBand is even easier when you understand the tools and settings available to help capture a perfect take

App used: GarageBand **Price:** £2.99/$4.99

Difficulty: Intermediate **Time needed:** 10 minutes

GarageBand lets you record both MIDI and audio, and each serves a different purpose. MIDI is a form of musical information that's widely used in music technology, and involves telling software which notes to play back, in what order, how hard and so on. MIDI in GarageBand is recorded by creating a software instrument and then tapping the relevant parts of the screen to enter notes at specific points. Interestingly you can also connect certain models of USB MIDI keyboard via the camera connection kit and play notes using this, if you'd prefer this method of input.

Your performances might not be perfect, and that's where quantization comes in. Quantization is when the software pulls the notes into the correct timing using a grid that you specify. When it comes to recording sound, GarageBand can use your iPad's built-in mic or a specialised audio attachment like IK Multimedia's iRig, which has a special guitar or mic input. We show you how to make use of the settings while recording.

GarageBand | Exploring GarageBand's settings

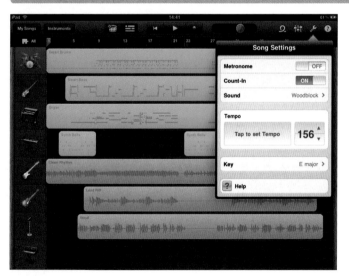

1: Open the Settings
Click on the spanner icon to open the Settings window. Turn the metronome on if you want to have a click track during recording, which is great for programming beats in the correct time. Also activate the count in to give you a run-up before recording.

2: Set the tempo
In the Tempo section you can choose the speed of the track by using the numerical field or by tapping the Tap box to set your own speed. Use the Key section to set the root key of the song – just tap on the key that you require.

Recording audio in GarageBand

Using the Audio Recorder you can set up and record sound from a mic, guitar or any other source…

Settings menus
Use the global and per-track settings boxes to change the fundamental characteristics of the song – its tempo, key and the effects applied to tracks, as well as using a click track and quantizing

Noise Gate
Use the Noise Gate function to cut off any sound that falls below a certain threshold. This is useful for making sure that when you pause between singing lines of a song, for example, room noise is not accidentally recorded

Audio interfacing
The iPad can record through its built-in mic but to record proper guitar, bass or vocals you will need a proper interface, such as IK Multimedia's iRig or the Alesis StudioDock. These provide professional level audio interfacing and microphone connectivity.

Audio presets
You can choose presets for the Audio Recorder module, such as small or large room, telephone line or even loudhailer. These provide quick and easy ways to affect the sound of the track to suit your needs

Use effects
Certain audio recording presets have effect controls. Here for example you can change the amount of compression and distortion applied to the channel

3: Set up a track
Select a track in a project and then click on the mixer icon at the top-right corner of the screen. For each track you can set it to Mute or Solo, show or hide its track controls and also set its volume and pan plus any echo and reverb that is being applied.

4: Set up audio recording
Select an Audio Recorder module and you will see some preset recording setups available. Click on the Plug icon at the top left to call up the Noise Gate, and turn this on and set a threshold level to cancel out all noise below that level such as hiss.

Edit your GarageBand projects

Making music in GarageBand on your iPad is great fun, but you need to know how to edit to get the most out of it

App used: GarageBand **Price:** £2.99/$4.99

Difficulty: Intermediate **Time needed:** 10 minutes

Transitioning GarageBand from the Mac to the very different form of the iPad was no mean feat, and Apple has done a remarkable job. In truth, although the applications share a name they are quite different to use, thanks to the touch interface of the iPad being so different to the mouse and keyboard.

You can record MIDI either by tapping the screen or by attaching a keyboard though the camera connection kit and record virtual instruments. Unfortunately as things stand it's not possible to edit the notes in MIDI clips after recording, except overdubbing drum parts.

You can also record audio tracks, and these clips like MIDI can be split and moved around the timeline, copied, pasted and cut to create your arrangements. As you might expect, the majority of the editing on the iPad version is done by pressing and holding on clips and choosing an edit function. For more advanced editing, you can send the project back to your Mac to be opened in GarageBand or Logic.

GarageBand | Master editing in GarageBand

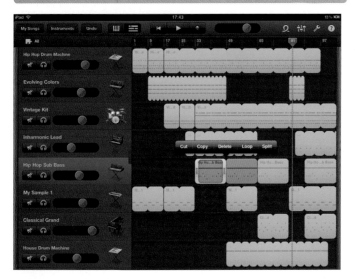

1: Edit a MIDI clip

To start editing a track, tap once on a recorded MIDI clip. From the resulting contextual menu you can choose to cut, copy or delete it, or to trim or split the clip. If it's not already looped you also get the option to Loop it.

2: Extend a loop

Once you have specified that a clip should be looped, you will see a circle icon appear on its right-hand edge. This can then be dragged to the right to extend the loop for as long as you like to create the exact sound you want.

GarageBand's timeline
GarageBand packs a lot of functionality into a surprisingly compact space…

Settings
Each track has a settings section, and you can control its volume, as well as its echo and reverb levels, to give sounds more space in the mix

Song Sections
Sequencing in GarageBand is done by building up sections of a song, each with a set number of bars. These can be managed using the Song Sections window. You can duplicate sections and modify them to create variations

MIDI clips
MIDI that you record into GarageBand is used to trigger virtual instruments, and the clips and loops arranged in the timeline. Unfortunately you can only overdub notes at present, not manually edit them one by one, which would be useful

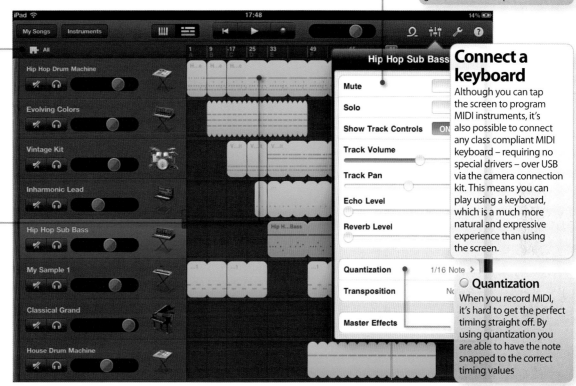

Connect a keyboard
Although you can tap the screen to program MIDI instruments, it's also possible to connect any class compliant MIDI keyboard – requiring no special drivers – over USB via the camera connection kit. This means you can play using a keyboard, which is a much more natural and expressive experience than using the screen.

Quantization
When you record MIDI, it's hard to get the perfect timing straight off. By using quantization you are able to have the note snapped to the correct timing values

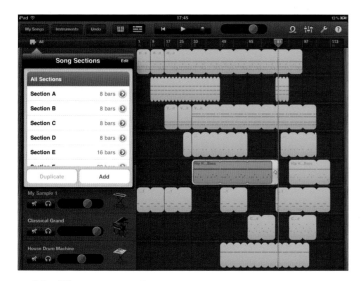

3: Modify song sections
Press the Song Sections button at the top left of the interface and you will then see all available sections. Click to add a new one or duplicate an existing one, and tap the Bars arrow to specify a new length that can extend up to 32 bars.

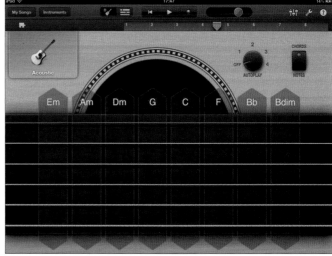

4: Edit an instrument
For any instrument or Smart track that your project may include, double tap on the track itself to return to the instrument's edit window. Then you can make any changes you may require to its sound or overdub a new MIDI part.

Master precision editing in iMovie

iMovie on the iPad 2 lets you edit the video you shoot with the on-board 720p video camera. You can also add music, transitions, photos and upload straight to the web

App used: iMovie **Price:** £2.99/$4.99

Difficulty: Intermediate **Time needed:** 15 minutes

The iPad 2 is now able to shoot HD video, and this opens up a whole world of new possibilities for those of us who love movie making. Apple has ported its iMovie software to the device, though it only runs on the latest hardware, so you'll need an iPad 2.

Capturing video is easy enough, though you aren't able to easily import videos from an alternative camera or from your Mac thanks to the way that iMovie encodes the video it captures. It's possible to save captured video to your Camera Roll, and also to send projects to iMovie on your Mac for further editing, so you can use these options to move your media around.

Editing is easy in the timeline thanks to the iPad's touch-screen interface. Clips can be dragged and dropped into projects, moved around and split, shortened and lengthened all with a few simple gestures. It's even possible to add stills with the Ken Burns effect to make your projects more interesting.

iMovie | Editing in iMovie

1: Move clips around

Clips can be dragged from the project bin into the timeline and once there, they can be picked up and rearranged by pressing and holding on them, then moving them to a new location. To remove a clip from the timeline you can simply drag it out and it will disappear.

2: Split clips

To split a clip, move the timeline so that the playhead is over the point at which you want to make the edit. Then tap once to select the clip and it is outlined in yellow. Swipe your finger down across the clip and it will be split in two.

iMovie's editing features

Fine tune your movies using these great tools…

Project bin
Here you'll see the clips that you have recorded on your iPad. Drag and drop ones you want in a project from the bin onto the timeline

Media chooser
Browse from your movie bin, your photo library and your music library to find material for your projects

Back and forth
iMovie isn't very flexible when it comes to importing video from other sources – it's very fiddly to do. It's great at exporting though, and gives you options to compress and upload to a number of popular video sites as well as sending the movie to iTunes, or as a project to iMovie on your Mac.

Clip handles
Drag the handle at the right-hand edge of a clip to the left to shorten it, or back to the right to restore its original length

Playhead
Place the playhead at the point you'd like to cut. Select the clip by tapping and swipe your finger down to make the edit

3: Change clip duration

To change the length of a clip, single tap to select it, and then scroll to the end. You can pick up the yellow handle at the end of the clip and drag it to the left to shorten it, or right to restore its original length. This only works with the right-hand slider, not the left.

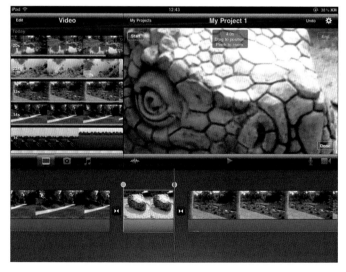

4: Edit a picture

Drag a picture in from your image library and place it into the timeline. Use the handles to change its length if required. Drag and pinch on the image to set the zoom level at the start and end of the clip, then play back to preview it.

Tricks

Use transitions in iMovie projects

Having transitions in your iMovie projects will make them look more professional, so it's a good idea to know how they work, and how to tweak them to suit your tastes…

App used: iMovie **Price:** £2.99/$4.99

Difficulty: Intermediate **Time needed:** 15 minutes

When you make movies, you will need to use some sort of transitions at some point. Basic cuts from one shot to another are fine, but transitions make things more interesting and help to create a more natural flow. As well as fades at the start and end of a project, you might want to use crossfades or dissolves between scenes, or some of the more complex transitions that iMovie has. Editing transitions is also possible, and rather easier on the iPad 2 version than on the smaller screens of the other devices.

Being able to control the timing of transitions is great because it lets you opt either for quick changes for a more urgent feel, or more slow and leisurely ones for a more relaxed pace. By double-clicking on a transition you open its editor window and are able to slide the handles to change its duration, as well as selecting from preset durations and selecting a transition type. Explore transitions to achieve a more professional look to your film projects.

iMovie | **Using transitions in iMovie**

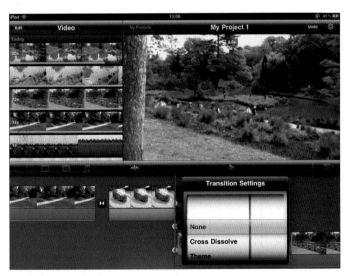

1: Set up start and end fades

Go to the Settings menu at the top-right corner of the screen and tap on it to reveal the project settings window. Here you can switch on fades from and to black for the start and end of the project, as well as choosing some options for the music.

2: Select a transition

When you drop a clip into the timeline, iMovie automatically creates a transition. If you don't want one, you can double-click on it and choose 'None' from the list. Or you can just leave it as the default cross dissolve if that's what you want.

Tricks

Transitions in iMovie
Master transitions for a better finished product

Timeline
Transitions are inserted automatically and also rendered in the background, so as soon as one is on the timeline you can preview it to see it played back, then edit it

Transition Settings
Control the transition here, choosing a preset length and a transition type. You also have the option to choose None if you want a straight cut to happen

Transition editor
Click on the dual arrows to expand the transition editor and view the way the clips overlap. Click on the yellow dot in the centre to open the Transition Settings window

Project settings
Tap on the project settings section to switch fades from and to black on and off for the project and also to choose a theme. The theme determines which transitions are available

Power hungry
The iPad version of iMovie only works officially on the iPad 2, and this is partly because of its dual core processor but also because it has 512MB RAM as opposed to the original iPad's 256MB. The iPhone and iPod Touch models supported also have 512MB, making them compatible as well.

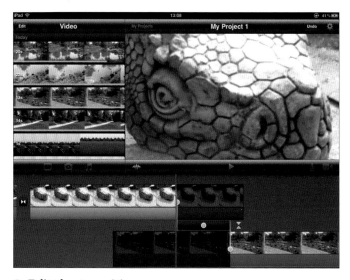

3: Edit the transition
You need to tap on the dual arrows by the transition to open up its editor view. You can then pinch-to-zoom in if you like, for far greater precision. Drag either clip to move it and so change the point at which the transition occurs.

4: Use theme transitions
Switch the transition type to Theme and you will use whichever transition is contained within the project theme. Choose the theme from the project settings menu. Scroll through the transition in the timeline to see it take effect.

Add a soundtrack to your iMovie project

A quality soundtrack adds an extra level of professionalism to a film. Here's how to quickly add one to your iMovie creation

App used:
iMovie

Price:
£2.99/$4.99

Difficulty:
Intermediate

Time needed:
10 minutes

To most people, the fact that iMovie exists at all is something of a triumph. After all, when you stop to think about it, the ability to not only record video, but also to edit it – and even export it to YouTube – is incredible.

But iMovie for iPad isn't just an example of how far technology has come. When Apple went about creating an iPad version of iMovie, it wanted to create a powerful video editor in its own right, not just a cut-down version of its big brother on the Mac. iMovie for iPad is more powerful than you might think – it just takes a while to learn about its power.

Take audio, for example. You're not limited to the audio track your recorded when you filmed your masterpiece. Each iMovie theme comes with its own soundtrack, which you can optionally add to your movie, but you can also add audio from your iPod app.

As well as the movie's own audio track, you can add a background music track and three foreground audio tracks.

iMovie | Adding a soundtrack to iMovie

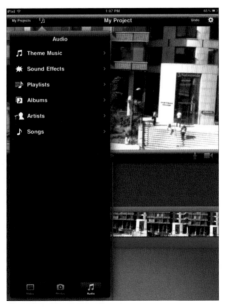

1: Use the built-in option
Choose one of the themes under the 'Select Theme' heading. Set the Theme Music button to On to automatically add this to your movie.

2: Add a sound effect
Tap the Audio button to view your options. Now, touch the Sound Effects button to reveal a choice of pre-built effects.

3: Adjusting audio
The sound effect appears as a blue bar. Tap the audio track, and drag the yellow selection handles to adjust the length of the clip.

Adding tracks in iMovie

Here's how to add some colour to your movie

iMovie's assumptions

How does iMovie distinguish between background and foreground audio? Simple: it treats imported files shorter than a minute as a foreground audio clip – a blue bar – and those longer than a minute as background music – a green bar.

● Recognising audio tracks
Foreground audio clips appear as blue bars in the timeline; voiceovers are purple, and background audio appears as a green bar

● Adding Theme music
You can add Theme music from the Project Settings window, although you can also add it from the Audio section of the Media Library

● Adding a voiceover
Want to add a voiceover? Tap the microphone icon, record a track, and it will be added as a foreground audio effect in front of the background audio track

● Background adjustments
The background music track has to start at the beginning of your project, and its volume is automatically adjusted when a video clip contains audio

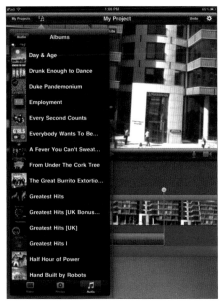

4: Add your own soundtrack
Go back to the Audio menu, and tap Playlists, Albums, Artists or Songs to find your favourite track. Tap the clip to add it to your project.

5: Delete audio
Changed your mind about the audio? You can select another track, though you can delete it by dragging it away from the timeline.

6: Adjust the volume
To adjust the background audio, double-tap the audio track to show a Settings menu. Here, you can adjust the clip's volume, or mute it.

Test your eyesight with your iPad

Is your eyesight as sharp as you think it is? A fun test can show you how well you can see

App used:
Vision Test

Price:
Free

Difficulty:
Beginner

Time needed:
10 minutes

Of all the myriad purposes to which an iPad could be put, it's unlikely that many could have foreseen a role for it as a tool to test eyesight.

But thanks to apps like Vision Test, an iPad can even check for eye problems, although it isn't designed to replace a visit to an optician (there are all sorts of problems that simply can't be identified using an iPad).

Vision Test runs a series of tests that involve checking your eyesight while holding the iPad at a set distance. The tests mimic those that an optician would run. For example, the app's Visual Acuity checks how well you can see objects in the distance, while another checks for the common problem of astigmatism – which can cause an eye to be unable to focus. A 'duochrome' test mimics those red and green tests you get at the opticians, and is designed to check for aberrations in how you focus, while another test checks for colour blindness. A short Q&A asks basic questions to identify future risks for your eye health. You end up with a short eyesight report.

Vision Test | Check your iPad eyesight

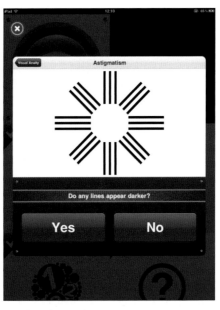

1: Visual Acuity
Hold your iPad at arms' length, and cover each eye. 12 letters are displayed one-by-one in decreasing sizes. Try to correctly identify them.

2: Checking for astigmatism
Again, hold your iPad at arm's length and cover an eye. The astigmatism test shows some lines; you must identify which ones appear darker.

3: Duochrome test
The Duochrome test shows an image on red and green backgrounds. Like the astigmatism test, say whether any of the lines look darker.

Your personal eyesight test

How to test your eyes

Tests complete
A tick in the corner of each test indicates that it has been completed, although you can run the same one again if you want

Test results
You can view the results of your test at any time by tapping this button

Good eye advice
Vision Test doesn't try to detract from the role of the optician – in fact, the app comes with several pages of well-designed eye advice to encourage you to take the health of your eyes seriously.

Find an optician
As well as tests, the program includes a function to locate the nearest optician to you – if your need for a proper eye test is urgent

Left or right?
The results will break down individual percentages for each eye, so you know whether you're stronger with your left or right eye

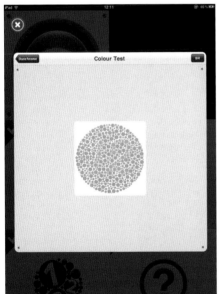

4: Testing colour blindness
This test displays four coloured patterns made up of circular dots. Identify the number that is displayed within these dots.

5: Final test
The final test comprises three questions covering issues that might affect your eyes. Answer the questions as truthfully as you can.

6: Test results
Upon completing a test, a short summary appears. These are stored for future reference, with an optician visit recommended if needed.

Discover your location using your iPad

We all presume that we know exactly where we are at any given time, but do we really?
You can get exact geographical location information with just an iPad

App used: Theodolite HD **Price:** £2.49/$3.99

Difficulty: Beginner **Time needed:** 10 minutes

 GPS is, of course, built into the iPad, and is ideal for satellite navigation. It is, however, just one location method among many, and there is an app that can offer a degree of location tracking that was previously only reserved for expensive specialist equipment.

Theodolite has its roots in professional communities who need specific data, but it is actually a very useful tool. It looks complicated at first, but there is a good reason for that. It has to display a large amount of information at any one time, and once you are used to the way it works, you will soon understand all of the data that is being presented.

The app can work as a compass, GPS, or a two-way inclinometer, and presents a varied selection of information via photos and screenshots. The imaging side is what could prove most useful to the majority of people, though some people may not think they need it. You may be surprised, however, at what it can do, and how beneficial it could be for you. In this tutorial, we will explain the benefits of the app, and how to make the most of what is included.

A myriad of information

What do all of the icons mean?

Targeting
To get the level just right, you need to move the iPad until the red box turns green – a simple indicator that means a lot

Just the data
If you don't need images, and are instead more concerned with the data produced, you can use the 'copy' function in the HD or Pro version to select the position, altitude and other results in simple text form. This makes it much easier to share the data with others.

Accuracy
The data displayed on screen is incredibly accurate, and allows you to make fine adjustments without touching the screen at all

Maps
The map functions are incredibly useful, and help in a variety of ways. Think of it as an advanced Google Maps

Camera functions
The camera is an important tool for collecting data, and is essential for displaying and sharing everything you capture with the app

Tricks

Theodolite HD | **Learn where you are**

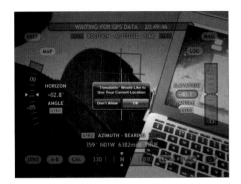

1: Start the right way
Click OK when the app asks if it can use your current location. If you click 'Don't Allow', many of the features will be unable to function.

2: The settings
Tap the 'Pref' icon in the top-left early on so that you can choose how you want the camera to work, and the units you prefer to use.

3: Calibration
Tap the 'CAL' icon on the main screen to calibrate the iPad. This is enables the various measurements to be taken accurately.

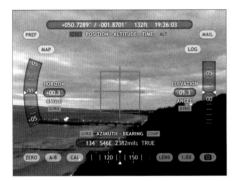

4: Positioning
You'll see a red square in the middle of the screen. Move the iPad until it lines up with the white cross. When it turns green, it will be level.

5: Mapping
Press the 'MAP' icon to use the mapping feature. Here, it will always show exactly what direction on the compass you are facing.

6: Clever mapping
The Rotate option keeps you facing in one direction and rotates the map as you move. This is useful if you need to follow a specific path.

7: Notes
There's an option to write notes against each photo. This is useful if you are taking multiple photos in one location.

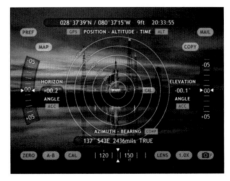

8: Taking things further
You may want to use the HD or Pro version, which offers facilities such as the Optical Rangefinder, which judges distances.

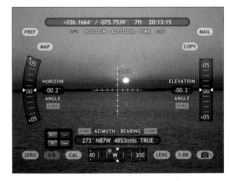

9: Low light
In the HD or Pro version you can use the Lens feature to toggle coloured filters, which help preserve the images in low light conditions.

iPad Tips, Tricks, Apps and Hacks **89**

Translate text and understand foreign signs

Translating foreign languages has just become easier than ever before, and this development could change many aspects of your life

App used:
Word Lens

Price:
Free

Difficulty:
Beginner

Time needed:
5 minutes

Learning a new language is never easy, and can take months or years of studying. Phrase books have long been the staple accessory for people travelling abroad, but now there is a new way. Word Lens can translate foreign words by holding up an iPad camera to the text, which replaces the words with a literal translation.

This technology can be used in many circumstances, such as reading road signs abroad, understanding menus and almost anything else. In theory, you could even read a foreign language book using Word Lens, but at the time of writing only English to Spanish translations are available. In total, it costs £14 for the translation both ways, so whether it's worthwhile depends on how often you need to use it. Hopefully, further languages will be available in the future, which will increase its flexibility even further. The potential is great, and the implementation is very clever, which means we may never have to worry about learning new languages in the future.

Word Lens | Translate with your camera

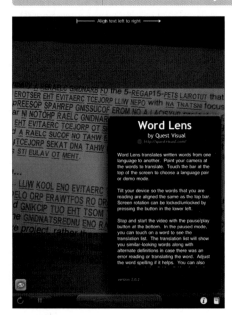

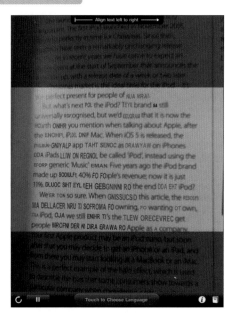

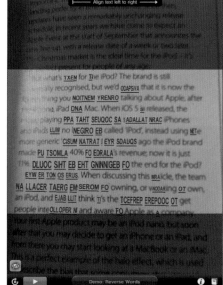

1: Getting started
When you first open the app, you should tap the 'i' at the bottom of the screen, which offers a simple explanation of how the app works.

2: Translate
Next, hold up your camera to a piece of foreign text. It can be on a road sign, magazine or anything else providing it is typed.

3: The results
Translated words are highlighted in blue upon pressing the pause button, as well as showing words that the app was unable to recognise.

The main translation interface

A look at the functions in Word Lens

Languages
Hopefully, in the future you will be able to select from multiple languages, which should cover every foreign trip you have planned

Pausing
When you tap the pause button, the translated words are highlighted in blue. You can check omissions easily, but the general meaning will hopefully be clear

Not too literal
No translation tool will be 100 per cent accurate due to grammatical differences, but an app like this should suffice on most occasions. If you still want literal translations, you will need to start a language course until Word Lens' software advances even further.

Camera
Unlike the iPhone version, options like autofocus cannot be altered when using the app, but the iPad camera can handle this sort of thing on its own

Manual translation
You can manually translate words by typing them into the app. This is a simple function that is similar to other apps, but works very well

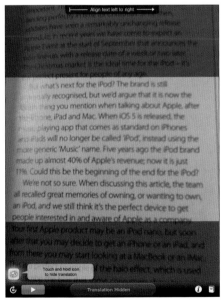

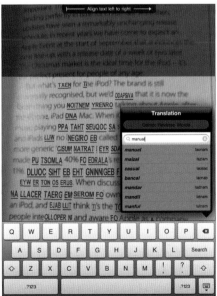

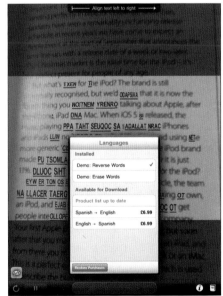

4: Toggling
When you tap the pause button, you can switch between the translated words and the original image by holding the Eye icon.

5: Manual translation
You can also type words to get their true meaning by tapping the far-right icon. This comes in handy time and time again.

6: Making it work
Tapping the bar at the bottom gives you the option to purchase two-way translations and to restore purchases.

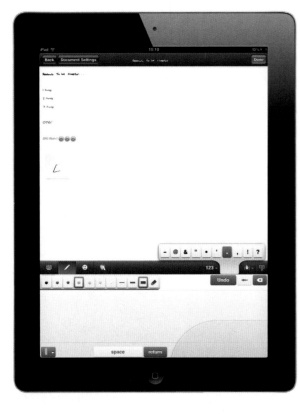

Turn your handwriting into text on an iPad

Keyboards are great, but nothing quite comes close to your own handwriting, and it is now perfectly possible to write on an iPad

App used:	FastFinga
Price:	£1.49/$1.99
Difficulty:	Beginner
Time needed:	10 minutes

Keyboards are the default method of data input for millions of people. The main problem is that they can be slow to use, particularly on phones, and don't offer the genuine sensation of writing. There is another way, however. FastFinga lets you use your own handwriting to create emails, notes and even tweets.

Despite the small screen size of the iPad, the app makes use of software trickery to ensure that the resulting notes are easy to read, and include as much text as possible. You can use your finger for notes or a stylus, but no matter what method you use, handwritten notes on an iPad are now possible, and in many cases preferable, as they add more personality to the finished article. For many years, there has been a quiet push towards making digital products work naturally with people who want to write notes, and we are quickly reaching the stage where the technology makes the experience feel the same as writing on real paper.

FastFinga | Handwrite on your iPad

1: Getting started
Upon opening the app, a blank page with a '+' button will appear. Tap this, and a new window will open. You are ready to start writing.

2: Start writing
Tap the pen icon, and use your finger to write in the magnified window at the bottom of the screen. Hit Enter to add your word to the page.

3: Use the thumb
After pressing Enter, the magic will start to happen. The text is made a lot smaller, and will appear in the note as normal sized writing.

Using your handwriting

How does FastFinga work?

○ Smaller text
No matter how large you write your words, FastFinga will shrink them down to a more realistic size

○ Tweaks
You can change the pen size, colour, and even use a virtual eraser while note-taking. The emoticons add extra personality

○ Quick changes
The arrows at the bottom let you quickly move around the note to insert new words or remove others. It is like advanced paper

Advanced settings
The advanced settings are well worth exploring, because they offer many tweaks that let you make the app your own. Everything from the shape of the pen nib to export image formats is covered to top off what is a surprisingly complete app.

○ Sharing and the rest
The arrow button takes you to the advanced settings and the sharing pane, where you can export your notes

4: Change the pen
You can change the pen size, colour, and undo your writing, or use the eraser to scrub out words that you no longer want to include.

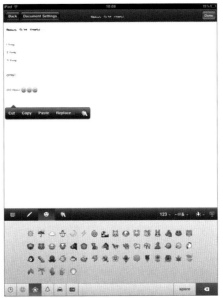

5: Add some personality
You also have access to a large selection of emoticons. Select the one you want to use, and it will appear in the note.

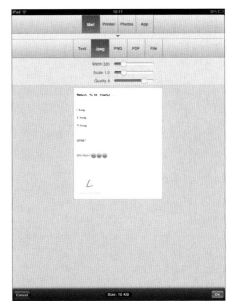

6: Sharing
Once the note is completed, you can share it with others via email, Twitter and Evernote. You can use your notes for almost any purpose.

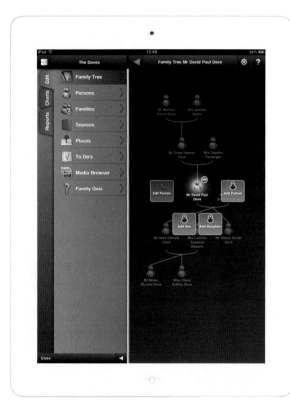

Create your own family tree

Trace your roots and start piecing together your ancestry with an iPad and a very intuitive app

App used:
MobileFamilyTree Pro

Price:
£2.99/$4.99

Difficulty:
Intermediate

Time needed:
20 minutes

Tracing your roots can be a fascinating process that allows us to discover the distant origins of our existence, and find out where our many traits, quirks and, ultimately, our names originated from. There are a variety of genealogy apps available for the iPad, and one of the best is MobileFamilyTree Pro.

You can edit your family tree, or use various practical reports to record your family history. If you own an iPad 2, you can even take photos and record videos. When launching the app for the first time, you simply give your volume a title, and are presented with a single representation of a person. Tap on this person, and options to add details appear. In no time at all, you can watch in amazement as your tree grows and takes shape.

Everything you compile can be easily distributed to all your relatives. You can print charts from within the app, or email them directly in a matter of minutes. So what are you waiting for? Grab your iPad, and find out who you think you are.

MobileFamilyTree Pro | Start growing your own tree

1: Start a new tree
Give your file a name, and select a function using the tabs and lists. To start a new tree, select 'Family Tree' in Edit, and add a person.

2: Add people
Tap 'Unnamed Person' and you will call up options to add children, parents and partners, as well as edit them.

3: Enter details
You can enter details about the person you tapped on, and even add relatives, which is a lot quicker than using the previous page.

Growing your own tree

Use the simple interface to track your relatives

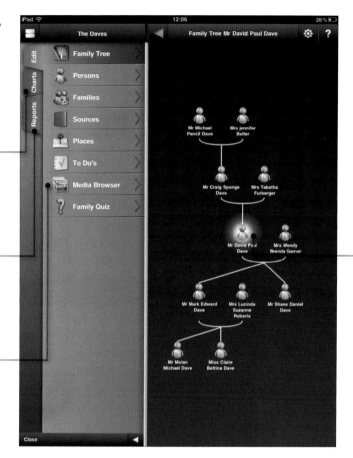

Change your chart
You can customise the look of your tree by tapping on the Charts tab, and then choosing a style to suit. Some may need a certain volume of entries to work

Check your reports
As the volume of info grows, the app will sort and organise it into reports that provide quick access on important info, like birthdays

Extra details
You can add other key details as you discover them, such as locations, sources and photographs. The app will even generate a quiz to test your family knowledge

One seed fits all
If you already use a particular genealogy app on your computer, then you don't have to painstakingly enter all of the details again when using this app. You can exchange data between apps on your iPad or computer using GEDCOM files. Tap the icon in the top-left corner to export from your device.

Your family
Tap on a person, and you'll be able to edit details about them, and also add direct relatives to be linked to them

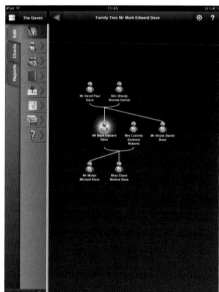

4: Linked up
When you return to the previous section, all of the people you entered into the tree will be present and linked together accordingly.

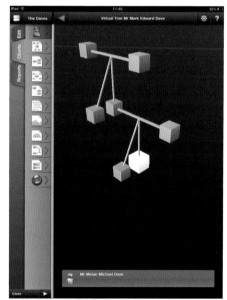

5: Change your chart
Tap on the Charts tab to choose something more to your liking. There are a wide range of styles on offer, from traditional to trendy.

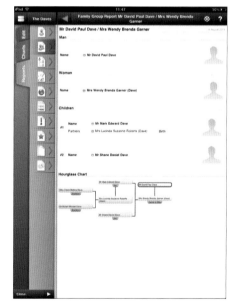

6: Read reports
By tapping Reports, all the info you have entered so far will be correlated into reports across a variety of different categories.

Plan and develop your own app

Got a good idea for a new app? Then start
building and developing it with App Cooker

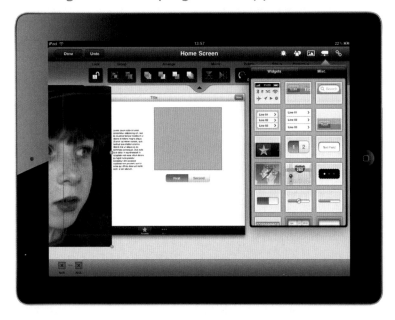

App used: App Cooker **Price:** £13.99/$19.99

Difficulty: Intermediate **Time needed:** 30 minutes

**All of the best apps are planned to perfection before
any coding commences.** It's easy to get carried away
by a good idea and lose sight of the fundamentals that
actually make your great idea a sound business. But what if you
possess a creative mind and not a cut-throat business one?
Mercifully, there is an app to help.

App Cooker is designed to support you through the five key
aspects of planning any mobile application: the idea, mock-
ups, the app icon, communication, and most importantly, the
business model. The app benefits everyone, from seasoned
developers to people who have the ideas, but not necessary
the nous to develop them, and an intuitive user interface will
allow you to get productive immediately.

App Cooker features a graphic editor that supports bitmap
drawing, customisable vector shapes and much more, plus
a mock-up engine that supports up to 99 screens and a live
preview. It's the perfect platform to nurture and develop your
ideas, and in this tutorial we'll run you through the basics.

App Cooker | Start building your own app

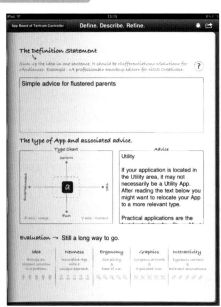

1: Start a new project
Tap the '+' icon to start a new project. You can
also name it on this first page. When you have
selected everything, tap on Create.

2: Define your app
Start by creating a 'Product Definition
Statement' for your app, which should clearly
define what the app does and who it is for.

3: Work out costs
On the 'Revenue & Expenses' page, you can
define and track the costs of developing your
idea and calculate the profitability potential.

Planning your own app

An intuitive interface helps you conceive and develop your ideas

Your App Board
All parts of your project are laid out on a creative work board for you to develop and enhance your ideas

Make suggestions
If you tap on the bug icon in the top-right corner of the screen, you can call up a drop-down menu featuring options to report bugs and make suggestions to the App Cooker developers

Tap to work
You can scroll through sections and tap on a panel to begin or continue working on that particular aspect of your project

Export your projects
If you tap on the arrow icon in the top-right corner of the window, you will call up options to export various aspects of your projects

Gathering goods
Although the app features a hefty database of tools and items to use in the mocking up of your app, you can also import items from other sources. For example, you can import images from your Photos app, or better still, link this app to Dropbox, and pull in additional elements from your cloud.

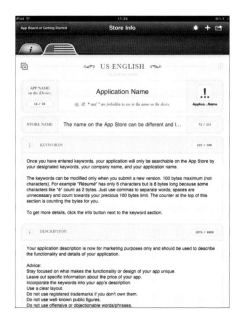

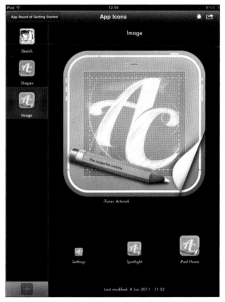

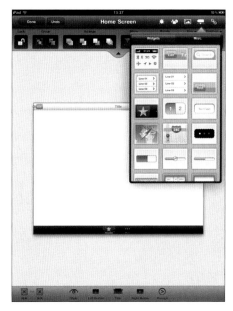

4: Enter Store submission info
The 'Store Info' page is where you can enter a full description of your app, give it a name, define the category and apply keywords.

5: Design an icon
There is a comprehensive icon editor that allows you to sketch out a rough idea, add solid shapes and then export it to other devices.

6: Mock up screens
Here, you can import images, use stock screen furniture, or create your own adornments from scratch. All screens can be exported as PDFs.

Hacks

Find out everything you need to know
about jailbreaking and see what's on
offer once you jailbreak your device

Hacks

Hacks

Discover how to unleash the full power of your iPad

106
Have fun with icons

108
Edit the user interface

132
Tweet with ease

The essential guide to jailbreaking

Ever feel you could get more from your beloved iPad? You could always jailbreak it. Here's everything you need to know about hacking your iPad

How do you jailbreak?

Jailbreaking is a process that's constantly evolving. It's quite possible that by the time this book is published, the current exploit will have been patched and there will be another way to jailbreak a device. Each and every exploit comes from a developer who has constructed a system where the device can be hacked. This either involves visiting a website and following the instructions or downloading a program that can perform the same task. The key factor is to ensure that you have the correct version of iOS on your device beforehand, otherwise you could do irreparable damage to it. We cannot stress how important this is. If the jailbreak is for iOS version 4.3.3, you need to see this value in the summary screen when your iPad is connected to iTunes. Provided you have the correct version of the software installed, you can jailbreak using the exploit available.

Jailbreak your iPad

The JailbreakMe exploit is the simplest, but it can only be used on devices running iOS 4.3.3 or lower

1. NAVIGATE TO JAILBREAKME
Open the Safari web browser on your iPad. In the URL window, enter the web address: http://jailbreakme.com. Tap the Go button on your keyboard to load the jailbreak website.

2. TAP TO INSTALL
If your iOS version is 4.3.3 or lower then you're in luck! Click 'Free' and then 'Install'. Your device will jailbreak and the Cydia app store will load on your home screen. Your device is now jailbroken.

3. USING iOS 4.3.5?
If your iPad is running 4.3.5, you'll need to download Redsn0w plus the iOS 4.3.4 and 4.3.5 firmware (do a search for them) to your computer in order to jailbreak. Unfortunately, this method doesn't support the iPad 2.

"Don't know what jailbreaking means? We explain what the process is all about"

What is jailbreaking?

Jailbreaking is the term used for hacking your iPad in order to install apps and settings that aren't allowed natively by Apple. A typical example of a jailbroken feature is the ability to change the icons that represent your apps. The reason people have opted to break through Apple's control of the operating system is that they believe that as the owner of the device they have the right to do whatever they like with it. Of course, jailbreaking isn't as simple as making the decision. It involves seriously changing the software on your iPad to accept jailbroken apps. There have been numerous ways to jailbreak and the process usually changes when Apple fixes any firmware exploits with each new iOS update. Once an exploit has been patched, the jailbreak community has to find a new way to hack the device in order to gain OS access. There have been some inventive ways to perform the task of jailbreaking. Originally, users had to create a custom version of the iOS software to load onto a device. Most recently, users have relied on the JailbreakMe website, which can hack a device with the click of a button.

Once you have jailbroken your device, you can customise the look of your iPad's home screen

---

"The key factor is to ensure that you have the correct version of iOS on your device"

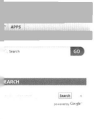

4. JAILBREAK VIA REDSN0W
Once downloaded, run Redsn0w and click Browse. Select the downloaded iOS 4.3.4 firmware. Once Redsn0w has processed the firmware, click Next. In the following screen, check that only 'Install Cydia' is ticked, then click Next.

5. ENTER DFU MODE
The device needs to be in DFU mode in order to apply the jailbreak. The on-screen instructions will help you do this. Once the process starts, do not touch anything until the task finishes.

6. REBOOT THE DEVICE
The iPad must be rebooted in order to apply the jailbreak. Repeat steps 4 and 5, but tick the 'Just boot tethered' box instead. This step must be performed whenever the iPad is booted up.

MacBook

Can you still use the normal functions and apps of your iPad?

Jailbreaking has no effect on your ability to use your iDevice as it was intended – unless you download an app that is designed to change those functions. You can still sync your device through iTunes, but bear in mind that the jailbreak data will not be backed up. This means that you can go about your normal routine with regards to iTunes, syncing music, movies, photos, backing up contacts and other information. You can also use the App Store in just the same way as you would normally do.

However, you do have to be alert when syncing to iTunes and its eagerness to update the software on your device. The method of jailbreaking is only valid for one specific version of the iOS firmware. Should you unwittingly update your iPad to a newer firmware version, you will lose the jailbreak and have to perform the process again. Even worse, if no jailbreak method is available for your new iOS version, you'll have to wait until one is created. iTunes will alert you when new software is available and prompt you to download and install it. You just have to remember to carefully read all notices, pop-ups, menus and commands.

Can I return back to the normal settings?

Reversing a jailbreak and going back to the default settings on a hacked device is always a possibility. It's one of the reasons why people feel it's safe to jailbreak their iPads and iPhones. Nothing is totally permanent because each new install of iOS overwrites the last. Thanks

to iTunes it's a very simple task to perform. If you wish, you can always go back to the original version of software that you hacked or upgrade to a new one. When going back to a normal version of iOS you will keep your App Store data, but any Cydia-related information

will be deleted. As we mentioned earlier, apps like AptBackup help take all the stress out of returning to a normal version of iOS. Should you wish to jump back into jailbreaking in the future, AptBackup will keep your Cydia data safe, ready for another bout of jailbreaking.

Restore your iPad to its original settings

1. iTUNES
Plug your device into your computer, load iTunes and then click on the device on the left-hand panel. Now click on the Restore button.

2. WARNING
You will now be prompted to back up your device before the restore takes place. This protects your data when the firmware is overwritten.

3. CONFIRM
Now confirm the restore. If there is a new version of the firmware available, you will be warned that your device will be updated.

How does it affect your warranty?

Jailbreaking your iPad will invalidate the warranty. In the unfortunate event that you experience a problem with your device (faulty speaker, faded screen etc) and take it into an Apple store, they may refuse to help you if they discover it is jailbroken.

Fortunately, you can avoid this situation by restoring your iPad via iTunes prior to visiting the Apple store. To do this, open iTunes and connect your iPad. Select the device from the menu on the left and click Restore. This process will reset your iPad to its factory default state. Be sure to back up your iPad first so you don't lose any valuable data.

This is also a very useful tool for rescuing the most poorly of iPads. If you fear you may have seriously broken your device while jailbreaking it, connecting it to iTunes and clicking Restore may help to bring it back to life.

Make sure to restore your iPad to the standard iOS before taking it to be repaired

Is it safe?

When you jailbreak your device, you open up the safety controls that Apple has carefully laid in place. You have to therefore accept the risks that come with jailbreaking. There have been instances of jailbreak viruses which have been able to take information from hacked devices. These viruses work in a similar way to traditional PC viruses, opening a script which talks to the owner of the virus, presenting him/her with the opportunity to explore and exploit your device; they will have complete access to all of your sensitive information.

Jailbreaking a device can also expose it to performance faults that normally wouldn't exist. In our experience we found that the iBooks application would refuse to load after jailbreaking our iPad. The problem went away the moment we restored the device to the default iOS firmware. If you're thinking of jailbreaking, you need to be prepared for potential unexpected problems.

Is it illegal?

The question that most potential jailbreakers ask is whether they will be breaking the law if they hack their iOS device. This is a tricky question as there are different levels of legality regarding the jailbreaking scene. First and foremost it is legal to jailbreak your device. In the eyes of the law, you own the device and can install any legal software you choose to. In the eyes of Apple, things are slightly different. The company does not view jailbreaking as an acceptable way to treat its products. As a result, should Apple discover that you've jailbroken your iPad, your warranty will be rendered null and void.

Beyond warranty issues, there are more serious questions of legality to bear in mind. These apply to the apps that can run on a hacked Apple device. Some

jailbreakers hack their devices so they can pirate applications from the App Store and run them for free. This is totally illegal and should be avoided. For those who are unsure, the default sources for jailbreak apps are legally sound. Installing pirated applications typically involves entering the download information into Cydia beforehand. When this happens, Cydia will flag up a warning regarding pirated software.

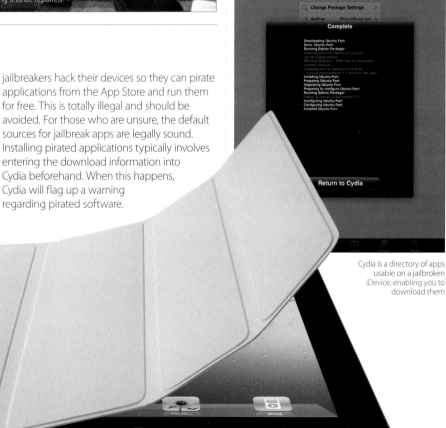

Cydia is a directory of apps usable on a jailbroken iDevice, enabling you to download them

While jailbreaking itself is not illegal, downloading pirated applications is, so be sure to stay on the right side of the law

What do you do if you 'brick' your device?

The term 'bricking your iPad' came about as the result of people's endeavours to hack their hardware. For those who were unsuccessful, their iPads would become frozen and unable to function. In other words, as much use as a brick. This can happen to anyone while attempting to jailbreak. Should this happen, you can try to save the device by setting it to DFU mode and restoring it in iTunes.

To enter DFU mode, connect your device to iTunes and hold down both the power and Home buttons for ten seconds. Following this, release the power button but keep the Home button held down. Eventually a symbol with an iTunes logo should appear and iTunes should alert you that it has found a device in DFU mode. From here you should be able to restore your device, although you may lose some data.

"Try to save it by setting it to DFU mode and restoring"

Where do you get apps?

When you jailbreak your Apple device, the Cydia app store icon is automatically added to your home screen. It works in much the same way as the regular App Store except that it's not quite as sophisticated. You can search for packages or browse through them by type and name. Despite the lack of Apple-esque sophistication, Cydia is both fun and easy to use. The types of apps available are actually greater in range and scope than those on the App Store. This is because of the lack of control over the supplied content. Hand in hand with this seemingly limitless scope is the unfortunate increase in the number of buggy and poorly coded apps. This is a direct result of the lack of policing that goes on. Fortunately, the best apps are extremely well made, very functional and easy to find with a little bit of online research.

Download an app

1. OPEN CYDIA
Tap on the Cydia icon on your iPad's home screen. If it is the first time you have done this, you will need to wait while the store updates and then reloads its internal database.

2. INTRODUCE YOURSELF
When opened for the first time, Cydia will ask what kind of user you are. Tap on User and then select Done. This will take you to the home screen of the Cydia App Store.

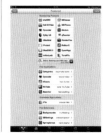

3. BROWSE THE STORE
You can now browse the store. The Featured section is a good place to start, as the most popular and useful apps are there. There's also a section dedicated to the iPad on the main screen.

4. SEARCH FOR WINTERBOARD
If you wish to alter the appearance of your iPad, you'll need to download the WinterBoard theme application. Either tap on the WinterBoard icon or use the search function in the menu at the bottom.

5. INSTALL THE APP
Each application has its own page that includes details on what the app does, recent updates or firmware restrictions, as well as screenshots. To install an app, select Install then hit Confirm.

6. INSTALLING… DONE!
As the app installs itself, you'll see a lot of code being generated on the screen – it may look scary but this is perfectly normal. When the app is installed, hit the Restart SpringBoard button.

Does it differ depending on what iPad you have?

Would-be jailbreakers have to be considerate of the version of iOS that their device is currently using, as it will determine the method of jailbreak used. The most popular method of jailbreaking (the JailbreakMe.com method) will only work on devices up to 4.3.3. Anyone using a device with 4.3.5 will either have to downgrade their software to 4.3.3 (a difficult and not always successful process) or use the Redsn0w method previously covered in our tutorial.

The downside of staying with 4.3.5 is the lack of an untethered jailbreak. This means that with every reboot, the device has to be connected to Redsn0w with the 'reboot device now' function activated. Without doing this, the device will be incapable of loading the jailbreak data by itself and will not fully boot up. This is due to the file system changes introduced by Apple with the update to 4.3.5.

The release of the iPad 2 has also further fragmented the jailbreaking process, resulting in different jailbreak scenarios across devices. A process that works on the original iPad may not work on its iPad 2 counterpart. At the time of writing, it is not possible to jailbreak an iPad 2 that's running iOS 4.3.5 firmware.

What happens when a newer version comes out?

As we've mentioned before, the jailbreak system is fluid. It has to be to survive the patches created by Apple every time a new version of iOS is released. Once you have jailbroken your device, that jailbreak will remain until you decide to either restore your device back to the same version of the iOS firmware that you hacked or until you upgrade to a newer version of the firmware. Should you wish to upgrade your device and then jailbreak again, you can do so as long as there is a hack for the newer version. It's worth noting that the jailbreak community doesn't jailbreak each and every version of iOS. They tend to only jailbreak major revisions rather than every incremental change. If you want to become a jailbreaker you'll need to get used to following the Dev Team and keeping a close eye on which versions of iOS are available and have been hacked. You will find as you grow accustomed to the system that there are trends of popularity in types of jailbreak according to the iOS version that is available. For instance, one method of jailbreaking will suit Mac users better than Windows users and vice versa.

Can you back up a jailbroken iPad?

You can back up a jailbroken iPad using iTunes as normal. However, the backup will only affect things that are legitimately on your device, so jailbreak apps and data will not be saved and restored for later use. Thankfully, there are jailbreak apps available that offer some kind of workaround; the most common is AptBackup.

Rather than create backups of the actual apps themselves, AptBackup generates a list of any installed Cydia applications and saves it within the standard backup to iTunes. Following a device restore or iOS upgrade, AptBackup can be used (following a re-jailbreak) to access that backed-up list and download any previously used Cydia apps in one fell swoop. It's something of a clunky workaround compared with iTunes, and one that's also incapable of restoring any previously used application settings. That said, it's still quicker than manually downloading each app again individually.

Back up your jailbroken iPad

1. DOWNLOAD
Search for AptBackup in the Cydia app store and then download the free app using the Install button at the top of the interface.

2. TAP IT
AptBackup will download and install onto your home screen. Tap the icon to launch the app.

3. READ AND DIGEST
The app is beyond simple; just read the instructions and hit the Backup button. The backup process should take no time at all to complete. You can do this at any time.

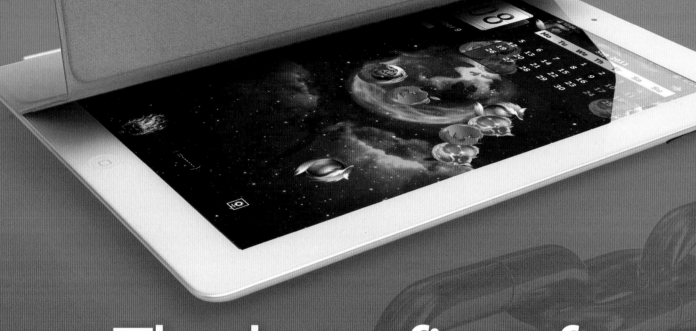

The benefits of jailbreaking your iPad

Discover a world of system tweaks, enhancements and apps that make your iPad faster, smarter and more fun

When you jailbreak your iPad you free it up to enable you to install programs that are unavailable through Apple's App Store. With no restrictions, the community of jailbreak coders have come up with increasingly clever and useful ways to tweak and use your iPad, although they don't have to comply to the high standards of the App Store. These range from system tweaks which change the way the interface works, to customisations in look and feel, to full-scale apps that let you use your iPad to its full potential. Read on to discover the various benefits of jailbreaking and find out just what you can do.

Configure icon spacing

Don't waste the acres of iPad screen estate – pack in your icons

So the iPhone comes with a rack of 3x4 icons and the iPad, with nearly six times more screen space, has space for 5x4 rows and columns of icons. It's not really making use of the available space and unless you are packing things into folders, there's soon screen after screen to contend with. Fortunately, having jailbroken your iPad, you can easily configure the icon spacing to either something more dense so they are packed in, or to a an actual shape of icons. The reasons for doing this is that there are a number of customisations that completely change the interface look and they require the icons to be spaced out in a specific way for it to work. The other reason is that if you have a nice piece of background artwork, it's annoying if the icons happen to land over important features. With a customised layout they can be arranged either aesthetically or to suit the background.

Pack the desktop with apps

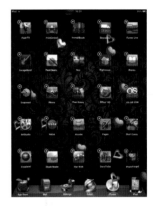

1. GET THE APPS
To remedy this waste of space on the iPad home screen, we're going to fill it with apps using Iconoclasm and a custom design. Firstly go into Cydia and enter 'Iconoclasm' in the search engine. Download and install.

2. GET THE CUSTOM DESIGN
Go into Settings and tap on Iconoclasm under the Extensions tab. Tap on Layout and select 5x5. You can also download and install other custom arrangements. Tap on the Iconoclasm tab to go back.

3. RESPRING AND REORGANISE THE ICONS
Tap on the 'Apply Changes and Respring' bar. Some of the icons will be on wrong pages, so tap and hold one to bring up 'jiggle mode' then move them into position to fill the screen.

Make more dock space

Don't be limited with icons on the dock – space them out

Perhaps the biggest annoyance for iPad owners compared to iPhone and iPod touch owners is the amount of space on the dock for your most-used apps. The standard six spaces isn't enough for non-jailbroken devices – but once you have, it's disappointing because you'll want to load Cydia and WinterBoard on there, as well as your favourite apps. Fortunately, one of the benefits of freeing your device is that you can both shovel as many apps onto the dock as you like and also make it either scroll from side to side to show more apps, or have it work in a paging system like the regular apps. The craziest thing, though, is that it's possible to have actual folders on the dock and inside those folders can be page after page of icons. Okay, so that's getting into *Inception*-like territory, so in this short tutorial let's look at simply freeing up that rigid dock.

Load the dock with apps

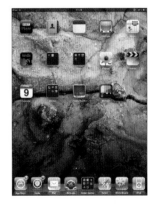

1. GET TWEAKING
The system tweak that we need for this process is called Infinidock, so go into Cydia and search for it. Once you have Infinidock installed, go to the Settings app and look under Extensions to find it.

2. SET THE PREFERENCES
Tap on Infinidock in the Settings menu and change the 'icons per page' setting to eight so that we can fill up that dock. Also, turn on the Scrolling Snap setting so that the dock snaps into place when scrolling sideways.

3. LOAD AND SCROLL
Tap any icon on the home screen and hold it to activate jiggle mode. Then drag icons to the dock. Once you reach eight, the rest will be shunted along onto the second page. You can also drag folders onto the dock.

Change your look and feel

Not just backgrounds – change the icons and sounds as well

While it's possible to change the lock screen and the home screen for your iPad, that's about it as far as a real change goes because you can't change the icons for the apps. You also can't change the layouts or what appears on the lock screen. Pretty soon it all starts to look fairly old. Fortunately, one of the main benefits of jailbreaking is to give the icons and system sounds a complete overhaul, which you can do with themes. There are themes for the status symbols at the top of the iPad screen, for the icons, the lock screen, keyboards and system. These are also really advanced themes that require multiple apps to configure and which change the user interface into something more like an HTC phone. These usually need the icons spacing out and quite a few tweaks to get the layouts right, but there are plenty of easy-to-use themes as well.

Smarten up that user interface

  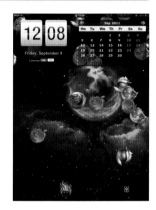

1. GET THEME ON CYDIA
We're going to install MobFire, which has new system sounds, status icons, an animated background, an HTC-style lock screen, new icons and wrappers for all the icons. Search and install it from Cydia.

2. GET THE REST OF THE TWEAKS
You will also need 60 Second Lock Screen, Lockscreen Clock Hide and WinterBoard, which is the standard for installing new themes. Get all these from Cydia and install them. Go to Settings.

3. SET IT ALL UP
On the settings screen, select Clock Hide and toggle it on. Tap on WinterBoard then Select Themes. Tap on MobFire (iPad) so it has a tick, then press the Home button to exit and respring the new theme.

Sort icons

Rigid patterns of icons are one thing, but what if they broke free?

As well as all the serious tweaks and customisations that you can do with jailbroken iPads and WinterBoard, there's some fun to be had as well. This means that instead of all those rigid columns and rows of icons, you can loosen things up on your home screens. There are various tweaks that allow you to mess around with icons so that the interface itself becomes either a showcase for what jailbreaking can do, or you can just show off what can actually be done. One of the most entertaining tweaks is to apply gravity to the home screen. Okay, so this sounds completely off the wall and indeed it is. With gravity being applied, all the icons will slide around the screen depending on which way you are holding it. This utilises the accelerometer to judge which way the iPad is being held and applies gravity to the icons.

Have fun with the icons

1. LOOK FOR THE APP
The system tweak we need for this kind of app icon free-for-all is called Graviboard. Search for it in Cydia and install. This also uses the Activator system, so that will be installed as well.

2. GO INTO THE SYSTEM
After installing and respringing, go into Settings to configure what will activate the gravity. Tap on Graviboard then Activation Methods. Tap on 'Shake Device' to select this method.

3. APPLY THE GRAVITY
For more fun, change the Finger Mode to Gravity Well, which will attract icons to a finger press. Otherwise, exit settings then shake your iPad to activate and send those icons flying around.

"One of the most entertaining tweaks is to apply gravity to the home screen"

Learn to edit files

Take control of the iPad filing system for the first time

One of the restrictions on the iPad is the lack of a filing system. This can be frustrating for some people, and in some cases can cause a number of issues. Two of the main problems are as follows; you can't copy files easily to or from the iPad because filing access is blocked. Connect it to your computer and only the Camera Roll folder is displayed, and that won't accept incoming files. The other problem is that you can't tweak the system or move files around when they are there.

There are two possible solutions to this using a jailbroken iPad. One of the options is to install a filing system app so that you can see the entire system and access it inside the iPad. The other is an external file program that can actually copy files directly to the iPad as if it were an external hard drive.

Delete photos to free up space

1. INSTALL iFILE
The best filing system app for the iPad is called iFile. This will grant you access to the entire workings of your system. Search for it on Cydia and install then run.

2. NAVIGATE THE SYSTEM
With iFile you can delete photos directly while out, without waiting to get back to iTunes to do it. Starting in /var, tap on mobile, then Media and then Photos.

3. DELETE THE HI-RES
Tap on the Thumbs folder then on one of the Fxx folders. They have a couple of hi-res images in each. Search for the one you want. Tap on it and select Image Viewer. You can now tap on the trash can to delete.

Room to view the artwork

1. GET STARTED WITH iBLANK
Go to Cydia and search for iBlank. Install it and run the app. Enter ten as the number of blanks required to space out two vertical columns on the usual four-column, five-row grid.

2. MOVE INTO PLACE
Although blank, the icons have a black shadow at moment so you can still see them. Tap and hold on one to go into jiggle mode then drag to the first screen to create the black channel.

3. REMOVE THE SHADOW
Once they are all positioned down the centre so we can see the background, press Home to exit jiggle mode. Go to WinterBoard and select 'No Icon Shadows – iBlank 4' to remove them.

Create custom spacing

Organise apps into specific layouts to suit themes or screens

As we saw with the icon-spacing benefit, it's annoying to have a rigid grid of app icons, especially when there's part of a background you want to be visible. Previously we showed how to create alternate patterns of app icons, but what if you want something specific that isn't available as a template? In that case you need to be able to space out the app icons yourself into the shape that you want. Unfortunately, this isn't as easy as just dragging them around, because the icons have to sit in positions on a grid. Now, you can change the format of that grid so that there are more or fewer icons on it, but the grid is still there. The solution is to use invisible icons for nonexistent apps. Welcome to the world of blanks. With invisible, blank icons, you can space out the ones you can see while filling in all the grid slots.

Hacks

Instant information

Keep up to date with lots of extra information on your lock screen

Unless you're using a fancy theme that loads up the lock screen with lots of interesting stuff, when you turn on the iPad you're faced with, well, a slider and the time. It's not very interesting or informative, although this has changed with iOS 5. Fortunately, this is one area where jailbreak apps have gone to town providing instant information fixes, weather reports, schedules and notifications. Most allow the information areas to be defined and organised so that the info you would like to see at an instant is brought to the forefront and the memo about gutter cleaning stays hidden in the background. For some of the more popular lock information apps there are also themes and additional plug-ins so the look can be customised or extra functionality can be added. One of the most graphically impressive is the HTC plug-in for LockInfo, while there are others that can add RSS, Twitter and to-do lists.

Renovate the lock screen

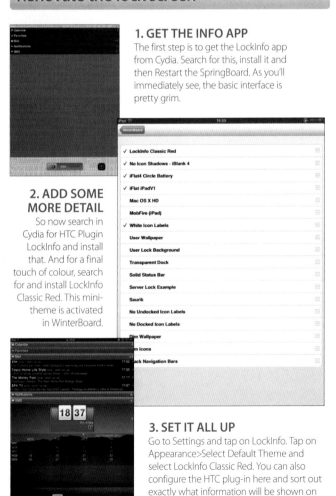

1. GET THE INFO APP
The first step is to get the LockInfo app from Cydia. Search for this, install it and then Restart the SpringBoard. As you'll immediately see, the basic interface is pretty grim.

2. ADD SOME MORE DETAIL
So now search in Cydia for HTC Plugin LockInfo and install that. And for a final touch of colour, search for and install LockInfo Classic Red. This mini-theme is activated in WinterBoard.

3. SET IT ALL UP
Go to Settings and tap on LockInfo. Tap on Appearance>Select Default Theme and select LockInfo Classic Red. You can also configure the HTC plug-in here and sort out exactly what information will be shown on the iPad lock screen.

Let's go surfing

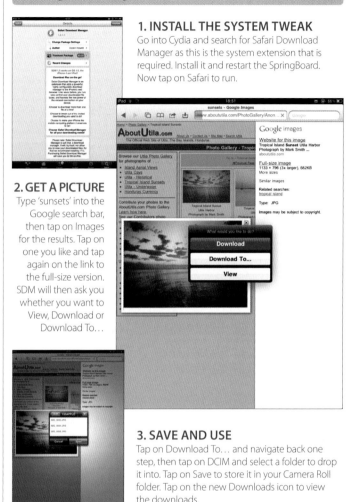

1. INSTALL THE SYSTEM TWEAK
Go into Cydia and search for Safari Download Manager as this is the system extension that is required. Install it and restart the SpringBoard. Now tap on Safari to run.

2. GET A PICTURE
Type 'sunsets' into the Google search bar, then tap on Images for the results. Tap on one you like and tap again on the link to the full-size version. SDM will then ask you whether you want to View, Download or Download To…

3. SAVE AND USE
Tap on Download To… and navigate back one step, then tap on DCIM and select a folder to drop it into. Tap on Save to store it in your Camera Roll folder. Tap on the new Downloads icon to view the downloads.

Download and use

Grab files and pictures from websites with ease

One of the limitations of the Safari browser is that it can't pull linked files off websites and neither can it simply download images you've found and want to use as backgrounds. When you throw in the inability to run plug-ins or Flash, you'll realise that mobile Safari does have its issues. However, by jailbreaking you can at least remedy one of these problems and that's the ability to download files with a proper download manager direct from the browser. It works as a plug-in so that it seamlessly integrates into Safari rather than requiring an entire new browser, so that any files you come across that have a hyperlink can be accessed. This means any media files and even zipped files. Any downloaded photos can then be used as a background image, while you are free to download work files and documents however you want.

Faster system access

Quickly turn on/off connectivity and alter system settings

The hub to tweaking and configuring your system is in fact the System app, which – on the iPad – takes on monstrous proportions given all the tweaks and toggles that are in there. Instead of wading through them looking for the right entry, just to turn something on or off, it would be much more convenient to have a pop-up configuration utility. One that was activated by a tap, gesture or swipe, rather than inside an app that you had to find. Of course, this is the premise of the legendary system tweak SBSetting which comes with a set of toggles for connectivity as well as allowing fast access to its own dock of apps. There's also the ability to not only kill running apps, which can be done from the multitasking menu anyway, but to actually clean up the memory as well.

Get toggling and customising

1. SET UP THE ACTIVATION
Search Cydia for SBSettings, download and install it. Then go into the Settings app and tap on Activator. Tap on At Home Screen and scroll down to Status Bar.

2. CONFIGURE THE OPTIONS
Tap on the entry for Double Tap and tap on SBSettings to select it. This will now be triggered when you double-tap the status bar. Exit Settings and do that now.

3. USE THE TOGGLES
Tap on the connectivity toggles to instantly turn them on or off. Tap on Processes to kill running apps and clear memory. Tap on Dock to bring up a mini-dock that you can load with system apps.

Sync wirelessly

Connect to iTunes, back up your iPad and sync without wires

It's been time-consuming to manually connect your iPad to your computer to back up and sync with iTunes, as with every other iDevice. Finally, the ability to sync wirelessly has been added to iOS 5 with the recent release. However, remember how long it took to get an untethered iOS 4.3.3 jailbreak? Remember how fast Apple patched that vulnerability? Well, let's just say you may be waiting a while for the first untethered iOS 5 jailbreak. If you don't want to lose all your great jailbreak tweaks and apps then you'll have to hold off iOS 5 for now, but don't worry because jailbreakers have been able to wirelessly sync for ages. That's right, one of the must-have jailbreak apps and tweaks has been to wirelessly sync accounts direct from the iPad. Note, though, that version 1.1 of Wi-Fi Sync only works with iPad 1; you'll need to wait for version 2.0 for iPad 2.

No more wires for syncing

1. YOU NEED WI-FI SYNC
There's a couple of things you need to set this up. The first is Wi-Fi Sync from Cydia, the second is an installer for your computer (Mac and PC). Install it from the following website: http://getwifisync.com/.

2. LET'S CONNECT
After installing the driver on your computer, run the app on your iPad. Note that it's an iPhone-size app. It will search for the driver on the computer and then pair with it. Confirm the connection by pressing the Yes button.

3. SYNC AWAY
The devices are then paired permanently and the wireless syncing begins. To sync again in the future, just turn your iPad on and tap on the Wi-Fi Sync app. It won't need to pair again, but now just syncs.

Create better folders

Faster, brighter, more colourful folders and folders within folders

It was a relief when Apple finally added folders to the iOS, especially on the small-screen devices. You might think that with the extra screen space of the iPad, though, that folders weren't as necessary. Well, yes they are and so are some tweaks to the way they work. Currently, regular folders have a thatch background that obscures what's beneath and they open fairly slowly. If you have an interesting background it gets obscured and also, if you're using a clever theme it will be blotted out. The folders are also a uniform grey colour and not particularly interesting to look at. Fortunately, there are a few jailbreak solutions to these issues which offer features like coloured/transparent backgrounds, coloured borders, folders within folders, and lightning-fast opening and closing times. It's only a small system tweak, but one which just makes it that little bit better.

Style your folders with colour

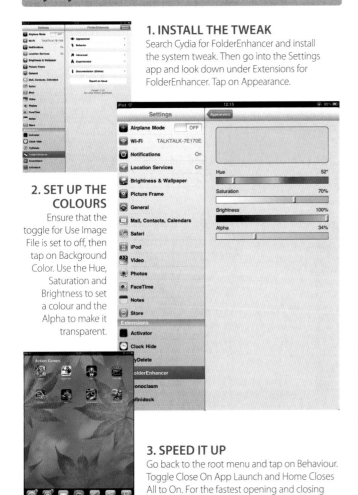

1. INSTALL THE TWEAK
Search Cydia for FolderEnhancer and install the system tweak. Then go into the Settings app and look down under Extensions for FolderEnhancer. Tap on Appearance.

2. SET UP THE COLOURS
Ensure that the toggle for Use Image File is set to off, then tap on Background Color. Use the Hue, Saturation and Brightness to set a colour and the Alpha to make it transparent.

3. SPEED IT UP
Go back to the root menu and tap on Behaviour. Toggle Close On App Launch and Home Closes All to On. For the fastest opening and closing speed, toggle Animation to On.

Remove and uninstall apps instantly

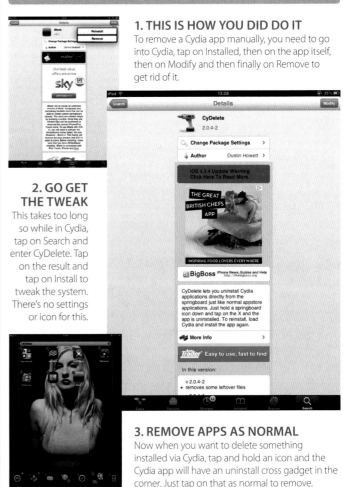

1. THIS IS HOW YOU DID DO IT
To remove a Cydia app manually, you need to go into Cydia, tap on Installed, then on the app itself, then on Modify and then finally on Remove to get rid of it.

2. GO GET THE TWEAK
This takes too long so while in Cydia, tap on Search and enter CyDelete. Tap on the result and tap on Install to tweak the system. There's no settings or icon for this.

3. REMOVE APPS AS NORMAL
Now when you want to delete something installed via Cydia, tap and hold an icon and the Cydia app will have an uninstall cross gadget in the corner. Just tap on that as normal to remove.

Removing apps instantly

Don't bother with uninstalling materials using Cydia, do it directly

One of the nice things about the regular interface is that to remove an app, all you have to do is tap and hold on any app until they go into jiggle mode. A cross gadget then appears on all the icons. All you have to do is tap on that cross to remove the app from your iPad. When you next sync, you get a prompt to either re-install or remove it from the library as well. Now, that's all well and good because those apps all come from the App Store. Cydia apps, on the other hand, are installed in a much more rough and ready fashion and don't come with an uninstall gadget. When you go into jiggle mode, any Cydia apps won't have that little cross on them, which means the only way to delete them is to go into Cydia itself. It's a very long-winded process when the whole point of jailbreaking is to speed things up. Fortunately, there's a jailbreak tweak for this.

Save YouTube videos directly

Download YouTube videos so you can watch them offline

The standard YouTube video app is fine as far as it goes. A chance to see those naughty Flash format files in fact, but what happens if you are out of Wi-Fi range? Yes, you can't watch anything, since it all relies on connectivity. Also, you know that the YouTube app only works on Wi-Fi and not 3G as well, so you either need to be at home or in a hotspot. The alternative has been to use computer-based web-browser downloads to get the files in MP4 format, add them to the iTunes library and sync them to the iPad. Laborious and you also still need to be at home to do it. Fortunately, jailbreaking offers much more fun and options with an app like MxTube. Now you can either stream the video even in 3G reception (if you have a 3G iPad, obviously) or download and save them directly for viewing later in a variety of quality and resolution formats.

How to download a video

1. GET THE MXTUBE APP
Search Cydia for MxTube and install it. Tap on the icon to run the app. Initially your library will be empty, so click on the Search icon and enter 'Green Day' for example.

2. SELECT A VIDEO
Tap on a video to select it and then either stream it directly or download and save into the library. There are Low, High and HD quality versions supported, but it depends on the upload quality.

3. DOWNLOAD AND PLAY
You can save multiple videos at once. So, having made some selections, go into the library to check on their download progress and then tap on one of the videos to play it.

Better displays for iPhone apps

Scale up those iPhone apps to use the iPad screen space

Although there are more and more universal binaries now that support both iPhone and iPad displays from a single app, you may still have a favourite app that was designed just for the iPhone. The problem is that when the 2x viewer is used, low-res iPhone apps look very crude on the iPad screen and also don't even fit the screen properly. This is because non-Retina iPhone apps run at 480x320 resolution compared to the 1024x768 iPad one. Retina iPhone apps run at the slightly lower 960x640 res on the iPhone, but appear as small-screen images on the iPad. When you double them they look crude again. Aside from hoping that your favourite developer upgrades their old app, is there anything you can do about this on jailbroken iPads? Well, yes. The RetinaPad system app makes Retina iPhone apps appear full-size and scales the text on low-res iPhone apps to make them look better.

Upscale your favourite app

1. DOWNLOAD THE TWEAK
Go to Cydia and search for RetinaPad. It costs $2.99, but note that it doesn't work on the iPad 2. Install it and then go to the Settings app and scroll down to RetinaPad.

2. TOGGLE OPTIONS
The RetinaPad app will have a list of toggles for supported programs (those present on your iPad) so that they can be switched on or off for RetinaPad help. Select the app you want from this list and toggle it on.

3. APPLY AND OBSERVE
This is a bit of a lucky dip as to how well it works, so exit the Settings and go to the app you are now using RetinaPad with. Run it as normal and tap on 2x. If it works it will look a lot better, but it won't work for all apps.

Move lots of icons at once

Select and move entire pages of icons at the same time

The standard method of moving icons around is fine when there's only a couple you want to move so they are all categorised together. The problem comes when using apps like iBlank to create a lot of new app icons, when you have a new theme that requires specific organisation, or if you just want to move everything around. The process of dragging icons, one at a time, from screen five to screen one is tedious, but for non-jailbreak devices there's no way around it. But when you have jailbroken, there is. A handy system tweak, MultiIconMover, does what you'd expect: it allows any number of icons to be selected and then moved directly to the page of your choice. There is a proviso, however, and that is that there has to be space on the page you are moving them to, otherwise they will stay where they are. It's still an essential jailbreak tweak, though.

Move multiple icons to a new page

INSTALL THE TWEAK
Use the search engine in Cydia to find MultiIconMover and install it. This is a hidden system tweak, so there's no app or even settings for it. Restart the Springboard when done.

SELECT THE APPS
Tap and hold an app icon to go into jiggle mode. Now tap all the app icons you want to move, but not on the remove gadget (cross). A tick should appear on the bottom-left corner.

GO TO THE RIGHT PAGE
Swipe through to the page you want to move them all to and press the Home button. If there's room they will all be moved at once to the new page. Press Home to exit.

Control your music files

Are you tired of iTunes telling you how to get music onto your iPad?

As we've seen throughout this list of benefits of jailbreaking, one of the big problems is that file access into and out of the iPad is heavily restricted. This is no more evident than with music and iTunes, where everything has to be synced in order to be played. The problem is there's only one iTunes account per iPad, so if you leave your computer behind it's impossible to copy music onto the iPad from another PC. One of the benefits of jailbreaking is to free things up so that music can be dragged and dropped onto the iPad and synced into the iPod library. You can also drag music out of your iTunes library and drop it onto other computers. An added benefit is that the Camera Roll can now accept incoming files, so photos and videos can be dropped directly onto the iPad and they are added to the Camera Roll.

Free up your music files

INSTALL THE NEW SYSTEM
The app you need for this is called PwnTunes. Search for it in Cydia and install. Now connect the iPad to your computer, but stop iTunes loading.

HAVE FUN WITH FILES
A new window will open on your computer showing the new folders for your iPad. From here you can add photos and video to the DCIM Camera Roll or drag music files into My Music.

COPY OUT MUSIC
Double-click on the iTunes Music folder to see all the music and video files that are on your iPad. You can now drag and drop these from this folder onto any other computer, sharing them.

Get Mac Dashboard widgets

Add the widgets from the Mac OS X system to your iPad

It's slightly annoying that the iPad doesn't come with weather and calculator apps like the iPhone, but it does mean you are free to find your own third-party versions. One of the more interesting ways of adding these utility apps is via the Mac Dashboard scheme. In case you're a PC owner, the Mac Dashboard is a pop-up spread of utilities like those mentioned, plus stocks and picture galleries and lots of third-party apps. It's like the sidebar widgets in Windows Vista, but they pop up and off on request rather than hogging screen space. One of the most innovative jailbreaks has been to bring the Dashboard world to the iPad with a range of widgets directly from the Mac. Some work, some don't, but half the fun is discovering what you can do with them. For this you'll need the appropriately titled Dashboard utility.

Add the Dashboard to your screen

INSTALL AND CONFIGURE
Search Cydia for Dashboard and install the app. Note that it's called Dashboard, not DashBoard. They are two different apps. Once installed, the Dashboard app appears; tap on it to run.

ORGANISE THE SCREEN
Tap on any widget and hold until it becomes transparent. Then you can move it around the screen. Tap on the little 'i' in the bottom corner of the weather app to enter your own location.

ADD NEW WIDGETS
Tap on the plus sign to select from other widgets that work on the iPad. Tap on the Find New Widgets sign to browse for new ones to install. Note: other widgets can crash the system.

Configure screen brightness usage

CONFIGURE THE OPTIONS
Tap on ScreenDimmer under Extensions and toggle it On. Set the screen dim time to your preferred time and when the backlight gets turned off. Toggle other extras On to save power.

GET THE APP YOU NEED
The app that can deliver this kind of battery-saving benefit is called ScreenDimmer. Search for it and install from Cydia – it costs $2.19. Then tap on Settings.

EXCLUDE SPECIFIC APPS
There are some apps that you don't want to suddenly dim. Tap on Excluded Apps. Toggle those apps to On which you don't want dimming out. Things like TV and navigation.

Control the screen brightness

Save battery life by configuring when and how the screen dims

There are two things that really hit battery life. One is continual use of Wi-Fi, the other is the screen display itself. Now, you can get your iPad to go into sleep mode after a set time, but that can get annoying. You can also turn the brightness down manually, but again, that's more effort than it's worth. Fortunately, these issues can be addressed and battery life conserved by intelligently altering the brightness, which is especially useful if you are out for the day with your iPad. It's possible to define when the screen gets dimmed, exclude specific apps from this, stop the iPad going to sleep while connected to a power source, turn the screen backlight off and tell the iPad not to dim the screen if something critical like satnav software is being used. Once set up, you can leave the system to carry on in the background, saving your battery power.

Create your own unique application shortcuts

Streamline your iPad experience by creating swipe gestures that dictate how your iDevice behaves. It's easy to set up with the free Cydia app Activator

App used: Activator

Price: Free

Difficulty: Beginner

Time needed: 5 minutes

One of the benefits of jailbreaking your iPad is being able to take your beloved Apple device and personalise it to your own requirements. For some people, the default iOS interface is all they'll ever need, but for those who like to get their hands dirty, there's plenty more to unlock in terms of potential.

Using the free Cydia app 'Activator', it's possible to determine how your iPad will behave following a particular combination of pre-determined actions. With a little work, you can set up a unique collection of shortcuts for your most frequently used iPad apps. These personalised shortcuts can consist of swipe gestures, button presses or even shaking the device itself.

It's possible to set up shortcuts that can be used either on the home screen, lock screen or within applications themselves. Given how Cydia apps are not part of the standard iOS infrastructure, Activator is an excellent way of integrating them into the everyday iOS experience.

Activator | Setting up a shortcut

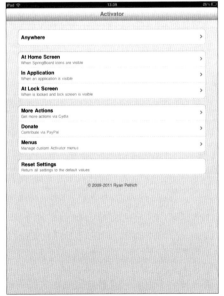

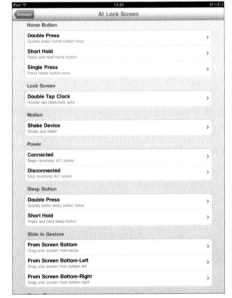

1: Getting started
You'll likely be able to find Activator on the Cydia homepage. Download the app using the standard installation procedure.

2: The main menu
Here, you can decide where you want your shortcut to be. We want our Cydia Marketplace shortcut on the Lock screen, so we'll select this.

3: Choose your buttons
Each menu allows for some excellent shortcuts. To create our Cydia shortcut, we chose 'Double Press' under the Home Button sub-menu.

Hacks

Setting up a shortcut

A look at Activator's shortcut setup page

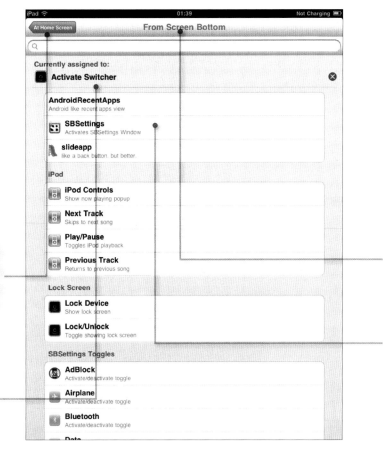

Even more actions

Beyond the many actions offered by the app itself there are also a number of additional compatible tweaks that can be installed via the 'More Actions' menu. These OS shortcuts are a mixture of actions that are used with Activator and tweaks that work in conjunction with other Cydia apps.

● Where it's at
The top-left button serves as a reminder of what aspect of iOS you are adjusting. It also takes you back to the previous menu

● Currently active
The first entry in the list will be of any currently assigned app. A simple tap of the 'x' button will remove the shortcut

● Taking action
The title at the top of the screen highlights the current action you are linking to a particular program or shortcut

● Control Cydia apps
Activator can do more than just control the standard iOS applications. Some Cydia apps are made with Activator in mind, and can also be added

4: What happens next
It's also possible to add iPod controls, system actions or app shortcuts. Here, we've selected Cydia.

5: Add more
It's possible to add more tweaks. We've added a shortcut that will start the Safari browser when the Lock Screen clock is double-tapped.

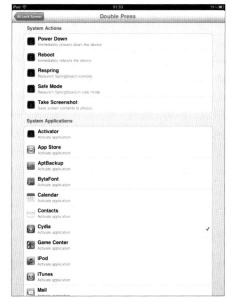

6: Endless combinations (almost)
The range of options at your disposal is massive. Activator can manipulate any installed app, and control many operating system actions.

Back up and restore your jailbreak apps

Should you ever restore your iPad, you'll need to find and reinstall your Cydia apps individually. Fortunately, AptBackup can do all the work for you

App used:
AptBackup

Price:
Free

Difficulty:
Beginner

Time needed:
10 minutes

Unless you're very fortunate, you will eventually have to perform an iTunes restore on your iPad. It's an unavoidable prospect. For standard users with a recent device, backing up isn't too much of a problem.

Unfortunately for those who prefer to jailbreak their device, this process isn't quite so desirable. While iTunes is happy to restore a jailbreak device to its factory defaults, it understandably doesn't support applications from the Cydia Marketplace. Following a device restore, any previously used Cydia apps have to be searched for and reinstalled manually. If you're used to having a large number of jailbreak tweaks installed then this can definitely be an unwanted, drawn-out process.

AptBackup is a free app that's able to streamline this problem by creating a backup list of your installed Cydia apps. This list is stored within the iTunes backup and is saved when your device is synced with iTunes.

AptBackup | Backup/Restore with AptBackup

1: Install AptBackup
AptBackup is a free download. To install it simply open the Cydia Marketplace, search for 'AptBackup' and select 'Install'.

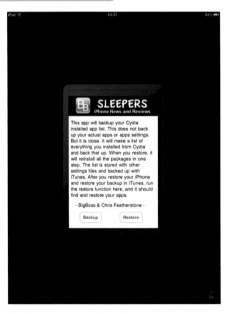

2: Create your backup
Once installed, the AptBackup icon can be found on the Springboard page. To create a backup, open the app and select 'Backup'.

3: Sync to iTunes
Now you have a backup file you need to sync it to iTunes. Connect your iPad to iTunes, right-click your listed device and select 'Back Up'.

Backup or restore?

AptBackup's important but oh-so-simple controls

An AptBackup alternative

If the limitations of AptBackup are a concern, a more fully featured alternative is PKGBackup. Unlike AptBackup, PKGBackup is not free or as easy to use out of the box. In its favour it includes the ability to back up applications to Dropbox, saving app settings in the process.

○ Backup

This is the Backup button. It creates a backup of your currently installed Cydia apps when you press it. This can be saved within iTunes.

○ Restore

This is the Restore button. Press this once you have re-jailbroken your iPad. AptBackup will automatically download and install all of your Cydia apps from before.

○ Compatible

Although this is an iPhone app and as such appears smaller on the screen, it is the ideal option to back up iPad apps too

○ Cydia apps only

AptBackup can only download apps from the default Cydia sources. Jailbreak apps from other locations (XBMC, VLC, etc) will need to be manually downloaded again.

4: Jailbreak it again

When you have to perform an iTunes restore, your iPad will revert to its pre-jailbreak state. You'll need to jailbreak it again.

5: Download, restore, reboot

After re-downloading AptBackup, open it and select 'Restore'. It'll take a few minutes, then your device will reboot.

6: Reinstall and reorganise

Once rebooted, you should find your Cydia apps waiting for you on your Springboard page. You will need to reapply any settings.

Hacks

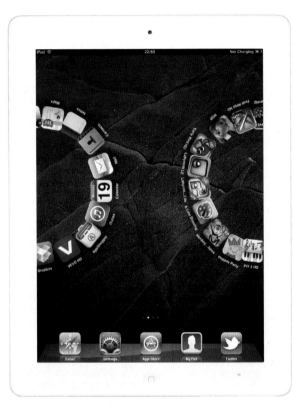

Install dazzling new icon animations

Barrel replaces the standard iOS icon swipe transition with 16 much cooler ones

App used:
Barrel

Price:
$2.99

Difficulty:
Beginner

Time needed:
2 minutes

Not everything to do with jailbreaking is about hacking the system's functionality or adding features that are traditionally locked out by the iOS software. In the case of apps like Barrel, it's really all about improving on appearances.

By default, iOS ships with just the single icon transition style. When you scroll from one home screen to the next, the icons move across the display to make way for the next page. Barrel takes this functional but plain transition and throws another 16 into the mix.

In terms of practicality there's nothing going on here that will help you be more productive. What you do get, however, is a new list of visual tweaks that you'll enjoy trying out. You'll also be able to show off your jailbreak skills to your friends as you flick through the various transitions on offer.

Whether you're looking for stylish fade effects, cube-based transitions or completely off-the-wall 'icon tossing' animations, Barrel has pretty much every base covered.

Barrel | Make home screens more interesting

1: Install the app
Like many of the most popular jailbreak apps, Barrel is available on the Cydia Marketplace. It isn't a free app, however, so there are differences in the install procedure when compared to the simple 'click and download' nature of free applications.

2: Make your payment
In order to pay for the app it is necessary to create a user account on Cydia first. This can be done with a Google ID or a Facebook account. The payment for the app itself is made via Paypal or Amazon Payments.

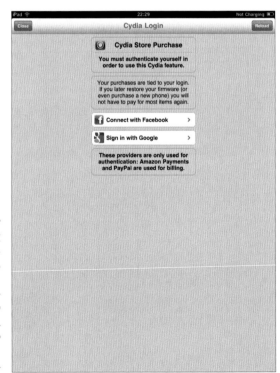

Picking a new icon transition

Barrel's simple interface makes changing icon transitions easy

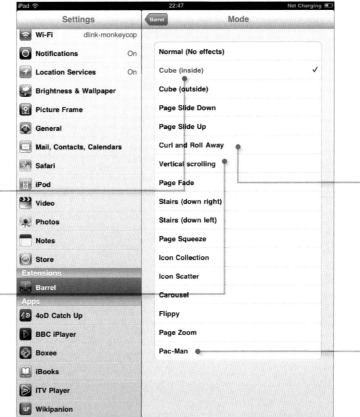

Beyond Barrel

Barrel is the product of uber-programmer Aaron Ash. Add **http://aaron. ms/repo** as a new source in Cydia to try some of his other apps in the earliest stages of development.

○ Cube

The Cube transition moves the icons as if they're attached to the inside or outside edges of a rotating cube. A simple but cool effect

○ Vertical scrolling

We like this one if only to confuse people when lending them our jailbroken iPad. The app icons will scroll up and down rather than side to side.

○ Curl and Roll Away

This is one of our favourite transitions. Moving the icons will force them into a wheel shape that rolls off the screen

○ Pac-Man

The Pac-Man transition is the newest addition to Barrel. It involves the app icons folding up into a Pac-Man shape and moving off the screen

3: Download and install

When the app is purchased it will download. The install procedure itself is like any other download process on the Cydia Marketplace. Once the app has installed it won't appear on any home page; instead it can be accessed via the Extensions menu in Settings.

4: Over a Barrel

This is where the fun begins. Pick a transition style and head back to the home page to try out your selection. While making your choice use the Home button double-tap function to quickly switch between the home page and the app itself.

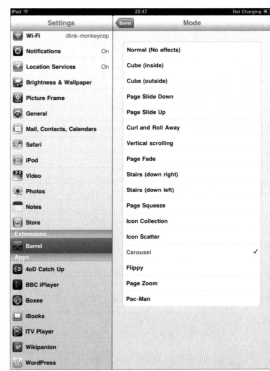

Add labels to your Springboard pages

Are your Springboard pages becoming messy? PageNames is a simple tweak that enables you to name your pages with whatever labels you like

App used:
PageNames

Price:
Free

Difficulty:
Beginner

Time needed:
2 minutes

One of the underlying themes of jailbreaking is taking the iPad interface and adding tweaks that make the iOS experience even more user-friendly.

Take page navigation for example. With our insatiable appetite for apps we're always on the lookout for new programs to install. More apps mean more icons, and as the quantity of installed apps increases, so does the number of Springboard pages that are required to house everything. It's possible to alleviate the problem by creating folders and placing app icons within them. For us it's something of an acceptable solution, but the downside is that it can result in endless rows of visually uninteresting folder icons.

But, as always, Cydia is here with a proper solution. PageNames is a simple Cydia tweak that adds a customisable label to each Springboard page. The traditional page dots are still present, but now they can be complemented by useful titles that explain the purpose of each page.

PageNames | Add labels to pages

1: Install PageNames
Open the Cydia Marketplace, search for PageNames and install. Once the install process has finished, press 'Restart Springboard'.

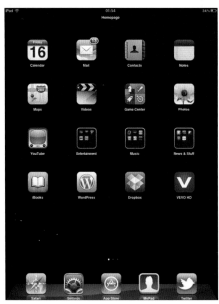

2: Pages with names
Once Springboard has restarted the effect can be seen immediately. Each Springboard page now has its own page number by default.

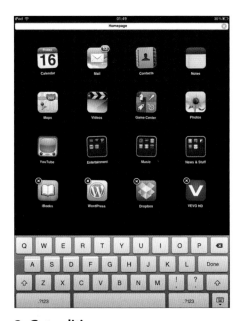

3: Get editing
Renaming page titles is easy. Press and hold on any icon until everything starts to jiggle. The title bar located at the top will now turn white.

Renaming a page

How PageNames works

○ **Hold to edit**

Pressing and holding on an icon initiates the 'jiggle mode'. The edit bar at the top of the page also turns white, ready for editing

○ **Rename your page**

When the bar is white, enter your new page name and press Done. Giving a page name an identity really helps to organise your icons

About the author

PageNames is created by Elias Limneos, a software developer for Apple jailbreak platforms. He has created a number of great tweaks for both the iPad and iPhone such as 'FoldersInFolders' and 'ScrollingBoard'. More information about his jailbreak tweaks can be found at www.limneos.net

○ **Plan ahead**

PageNames can rename your pages but it cannot reorganise them. Plan your Springboard layout ahead of time to avoid moving entire pages of icons around

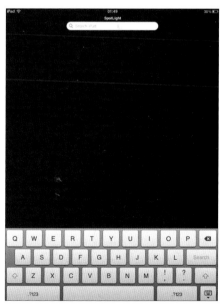

4: Name it

Tap on the bar and the keyboard will appear. Enter the name and press 'Done'. If you don't press Done your changes won't be saved.

5: Jiggle and edit

To save time you can flick between pages while staying in 'jiggle mode' and edit more than one page. As before, remember to press Done.

6: A fixed Spotlight

It's useful being able to set up your own page names, but unfortunately the Spotlight page is locked and cannot be edited with PageNames.

Multitask in your iPad applications with ease

Drop the standard iOS multitasker in favour of something with a bit more kick. Multifl0w brings the best of previous app-switchers to the iPad

App used:
Multifl0w

Price:
$4.99

Difficulty:
Beginner

Time needed:
5 minutes

Before the days of iOS 4, the only method of multitasking your running programs was to jailbreak your device and install an application such as Backgrounder. With the release of iOS 4.2, multitasking became a reality for every iPad user regardless of their device's jailbreak status. Despite this, the groundwork has already been laid by the jailbreak applications that have come before. One such app is Multifl0w, which has seen a recent upgrade.

Multifl0w is a slick multitasker app that can handle up to nine previously used applications. It can be activated by the standard Home button double-press or used in conjunction with Activator to create a unique activation gesture.

At $4.99 Multifl0w may seem a touch expensive for a function that you already have, but you're really paying for the slick interface. Ultimately, it is for you to decide whether you'll really get enough use of it to justify the cost.

Multifl0w | Switching apps with Multifl0w

1: Install Multifl0w
The Multifl0w app is available from the standard Cydia Marketplace sources and carries a $4.99 charge. Start by installing it.

2: Multifl0w settings
Multifl0w's home can be found within the Extensions section of the settings menu. Tap it to open the app settings.

3: Get activated
At the top of the Multifl0w settings screen, tap Activation Methods to open up a list of key presses that can open the application.

Setting up Multifl0w

This magnificent multitasker contains a large number of settings

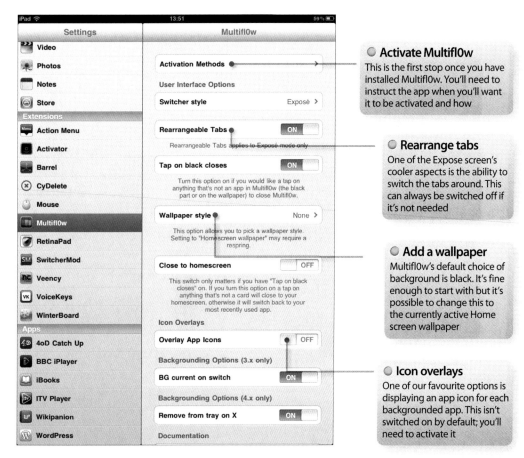

Multitask the multitaskers

It's possible to use Multifl0w alongside the standard iOS task switcher if you'd like to have the choice. Simply deactivate the 'Home button double tap' setting in the Activator menu. There's also a ton of useful information on how Multifl0w handles apps on the official FAQ at www.multifl0w.com/faq.

Activate Multifl0w
This is the first stop once you have installed Multifl0w. You'll need to instruct the app when you'll want it to be activated and how

Rearrange tabs
One of the Expose screen's cooler aspects is the ability to switch the tabs around. This can always be switched off if it's not needed

Add a wallpaper
Multifl0w's default choice of background is black. It's fine enough to start with but it's possible to change this to the currently active Home screen wallpaper

Icon overlays
One of our favourite options is displaying an app icon for each backgrounded app. This isn't switched on by default; you'll need to activate it

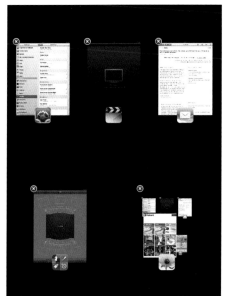

4: Get switching
Open and close a handful of apps then trigger your activation method. The app will kick in and you can choose to go into any displayed app.

5: Shuffle the deck
It's also possible to move any multitasked apps around when Multifl0w is in Expose mode. All it takes is a simple press and hold.

6: Expose vs Cards
There are two different modes of multitasking: Expose & Cards. Cards lacks the flair of Expose but the screen grabs are much bigger.

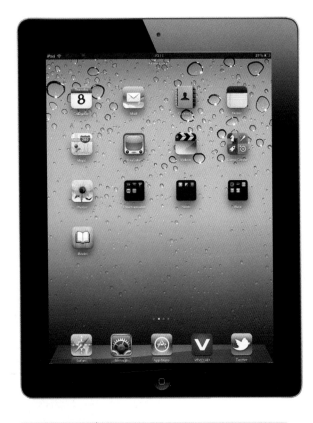

Install a new system font on your iPad

Apply a new font to bring a fresh new look to a tired old iOS interface. It's an easy tweak to perform thanks to BytaFont

App used:
BytaFont

Price:
Free

Difficulty:
Beginner

Time needed:
5 minutes

Fonts are one of the most important features of any user interface. They help form a user's first impressions when trying an operating system for the first time, so they have to be correct from the off. The perfect font should be attractive to the eye and comfortable to read, but it mustn't be distracting. If a font takes the user's mind away from the task in hand then it is doing something wrong.

The default font choice for the iPad is a typical example of the perfect font – that's no surprise given the amount of work Apple has put into the finer details of its operating system. But some users will still have a niggling itch to change the default system font to something they prefer. This is a feature that is not offered as standard on iOS. Anyone who wants to mess about with their fonts has to go the way of the jailbreak. Available on the Cydia Marketplace is BytaFont, a free download that offers the user the ability to swap out system fonts for any available replacement of their choice.

BytaFont | Change your system font

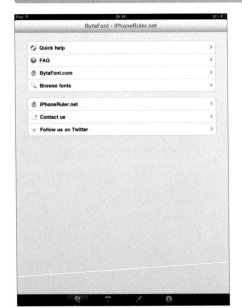

1: Browse for fonts
Changing fonts is a simple enough process. Once you've installed the app, open it and select 'Browse fonts'.

2: Where to start?
BytaFont packs over 400 fonts. The 'Staff picks' section is a good place to start, although the Categories section is also worth a look.

3: Preview and install
Selecting a font title will open up a preview gallery. If you wish to install it simply click 'Install via Cydia' and the font will install.

The BytaFont font menu

How to apply fonts in BytaFont

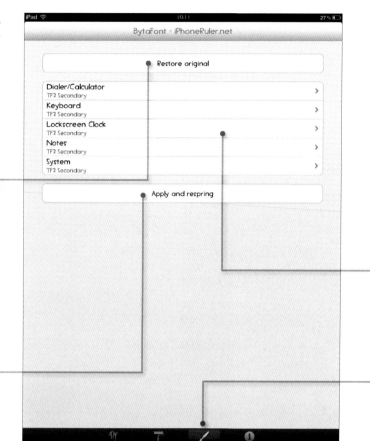

Change font sizes

Picking an ideal font may take some time, especially with so many to choose from. You may also run into the perfect font but find that it's too big to be practical. If you need to adjust the size of your font then Shrink is a Cydia app that can do this along with changing the size of your Springboard icons.

● Reverse your changes

There's no need to worry about losing your default iPad fonts. BytaFont automatically makes a backup file that can be applied by pressing this button

● Localise your changes

BytaFont makes it possible to apply different fonts to varying aspects of the user interface. Click an option here to open up the font menu

● Apply and respring

Once you've finished making your changes to the various parts of the operating system you can apply them all at once by using this button

● The menu buttons

Considering the system-wide changes BytaFont makes, it's a surprisingly simple little program with only a few screens to flick through

4: Apply your font

Go back to BytaFont and select Basic. A list of fonts will appear. Click on your downloaded font, select Yes to respring and apply the font.

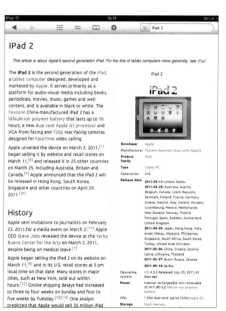

5: See the results

Your device will restart with its new look. You can apply different fonts to different aspects of your device in the Advanced menu in BytaFont.

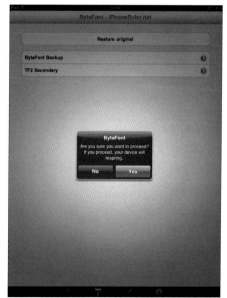

6: Restore the originals

If you wish to go back to how things were then select 'Restore Original' in the Basic menu. The default font will install once you click on Yes.

Hacks

Stream your movie collection to your iPad

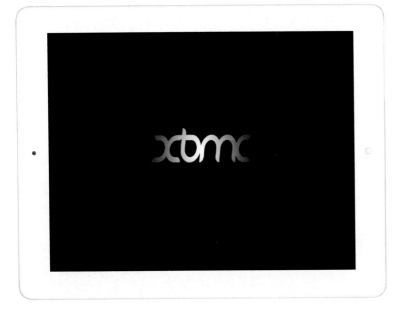

The popular home theatre software XBMC has come to iOS. We take a look at how it can turn your iPad into the perfect wireless media hub

App used: XBMC Price: Free

Difficulty: Expert Time needed: 30 minutes

XBMC (formerly known as Xbox Media Center) began life as a media player for the Xbox games console. Over the years the software has found its way onto various desktop platforms and most recently on portable iOS devices. Due to its open source nature it's not possible to download XBMC via the App Store. The only way to obtain it is via Cydia on a jailbroken device.

When used in conjunction with a computer running XBMC, your iPad is able to perform the functions of a wireless media receiver. Movies can be chosen from your stored collection and streamed directly to your device.

Using XBMC on an iPad can be a disorientating experience at first. The app doesn't follow the expected swipe gestures of other apps; it adopts a mouse pointer interface that imitates the controls of its computer counterparts. Tapping on an item will select it, double tapping will replicate a right click and swiping to the left will move the app back a page.

In order to use XBMC for media streaming you will also need to have it installed on your desktop computer.

Watching a video
A look at video playback on XBMC

Subtitles
The four small icons along the bottom of the screen allow access to the playback setting of XBMC. Clicking the first icon enables subtitles

Tap the screen
Tapping the screen during playback will display the movie player controls. A close dialog box is also included in the top right of the screen

Video settings
The movie reel icon brings up the Video Settings menu. There are some fairly advanced options available in here so be careful of any changes made

Stream from elsewhere
XBMC doesn't just limit you to the media you have stored locally. There's also YouTube support and a range of free media add-ons to download. Many of these take the form of TV channels from the likes of Engadget or Cnet that reside in your video library, offering you media clips to stream online.

Bookmark a scene
XBMC also includes bookmarks. At your chosen moment tap the page icon followed by Create Bookmark. XBMC will save the current time and a screenshot

XBMC | Stream movies to iPad

1: Install XBMC
The source must be added to Cydia's sources list. In Cydia, press Sources>Edit>Add and enter http://mirrors.xbmc.org/apt/ios.

2: Navigating the UI
The default home screen features a scroll bar. Tapping a function will select it. Using two fingers will bring up a mouse pointer.

3: Add video files
Open XBMC and tap Files>Browse>UPnP Devices>XBMC: Media Server>Video Library>Movies>Title to select where to stream from.

4: Grab that metadata
XBMC uses a metadata scraper to get info about your movie files. Select Movies from the top menu, tag Automated Scan and click OK.

5: View your library
At the main screen tap Library>Files>XBMC: Media Server to open your movie list. Tapping a movie initiates playback.

6: Video playback
Tapping the screen during playback will display the control panel and general playback settings for XBMC.

7: More than movies
It's possible to set up streaming galleries for your music and photo collections. You still need to have XBMC running on your other device.

8: Change the skin
You can also alter the appearance of the app. Tap Settings>Appearance>Skin>Get More, then choose a new look and install it.

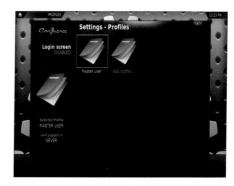

9: Create user profiles
XBMC also supports multiple user profiles. Each user can set their own security settings, choose their own skin and media libraries.

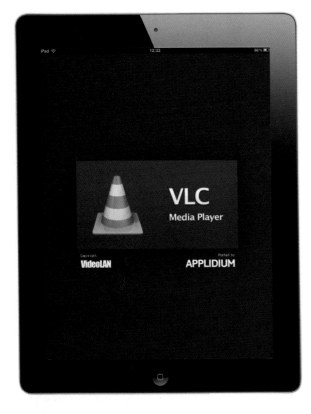

View a range of files directly on your iPad

Formerly available on the App Store, VLC plays almost anything you throw at it

App used:
VLC Media Player

Price:
Free

Difficulty:
Intermediate

Time needed:
20 minutes

VLC Media Player has been on the receiving end of a somewhat bumpy ride with regards to its iOS debut. Originally it was available for free on the App Store but the developers soon pulled it due to legal complications regarding VLC's open source nature.

VLC is a free media player that boasts support for almost every video file within its simple yet powerful interface. For anyone with a large collection of DivX files VLC will happily play these back on your device without the need for converting beforehand. Although sadly the support isn't quite there for true HD material.

Unfortunately, the loss of its App Store status has also resulted in VLC losing support in iTunes. Previously it was possible to sync video files with a mouse click. Now, in order to copy movies to your iPad it needs to be done via an FTP connection. It's not a difficult task to perform but it's certainly less than convenient.

VLC Media Player | Play videos on VLC

1: Add new source
Installing VLC takes a little more work than a standard Cydia install. We need to tell Cydia where to download VLC from.

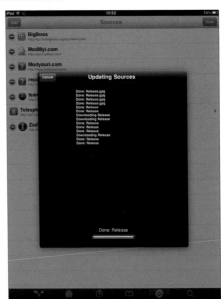

2: Download VLC
Press Edit>Add and enter **http://rpetri.ch/repo**. Tap Add Source. Tap Done and search for VLC. Download the app as normal.

3: Install OpenSSH
To be able to transfer videos from your computer to your iPad you will also need to install OpenSSH. Search for this and install it.

Navigating the VLC gallery page

A look at the simple yet effective VLC interface

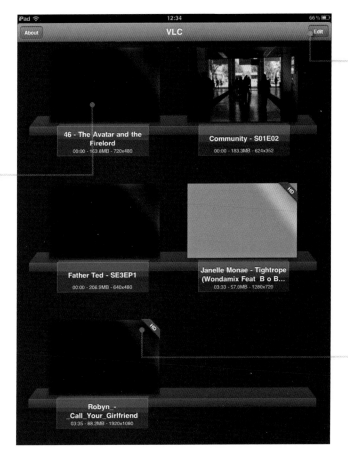

Video info
Any videos found by VLC are displayed with an image and information about the file itself

Deleting videos
Videos can be removed directly from the app. Click on the Edit button and tap the small red cross that appears next to each entry

Not HD ready
VLC will pick up on HD content but it won't be keen to play it. A warning will appear should you try to play some

Alternatives to VLC

VLC is a one-of-a-kind program; there isn't anything else for the iPad that can handle as many formats in one package. It's a shame that getting files into it can be so time consuming. The App Store has a couple of official alternatives in the form of CineXplayer and yxplayer. Unlike VLC, these apps are not free.

4: FTP and IP
You'll need an FTP program to transfer videos. On the iPad tap Settings>Wi-Fi and select your network to find out your iPad's IP address.

5: Upload your videos
Enter this IP address into the Host box on your FTP client. Log in to your iPad and upload your videos to /private/var/mobile/Media.

6: Ready for playback
Once the upload has finished the videos will appear in VLC ready for playback. Tapping a video will start the playback.

Hacks

Stay connected to Facebook and Twitter

qTweeter's instant-access drop-down update window puts the social network at your fingertips

App used:
qTweeter

Price:
Free trial, $3.99
thereafter

Difficulty:
Beginner

Time needed:
5 minutes

qTweeter pitches itself as the fastest and most efficient way to use Twitter and update your Facebook status. Its main mechanic is a drop-down window that sits hidden at the top of any application in use. Simply drag down the window, type your status update and then swipe it away again without ever leaving your current app.

For such a small app, qTweeter does a great job of including the same kind of functionality found in much larger Twitter clients. Along with simultaneous Facebook and Twitter updates it's also possible to upload images, videos, links and your current location. There's also multi-account support, over-long tweet handling and image previews.

While the app doesn't overtly claim to support the iPad, we managed to install it to our device with no problems; however, we did suffer the odd glitch while using the app. To its credit qTweeter includes a useful free trial that lasts for a number of updates. This should give you a good idea of whether qTweeter is ideal for your social networking requirements.

---

qTweeter | Set up qTweeter for Twitter

1: Download qTweeter
qTweeter is easily found on the Cydia Marketplace. Despite being a paid app it also includes a limited free trial.

2: The main menu
The main qTweeter menu is clearly laid out and intuitive to follow. To connect to a network tap on 'Add Account'.

3: Authorise your account
qTweeter allows Twitter and Facebook accounts. Both include the official authentication processes so your details are safe.

Tweeting directly from the homepage

Using qTweeter's compact but useful interface

○ **Which account?**
You can post to any number of accounts that have been set up in qTweeter. Tap the avatar to decide which accounts will be updated

Your own unique look
If the standard blue-coloured box of qTweeter is a bit bland for your tastes you can apply a custom background from the Settings menu. You can use any picture from your gallery or snap a picture from a camera should your device have one.

○ **What is #nowplaying**
With iTunes running in the background, open qTweeter and tap on the musical note icon. qTweeter will post an update of what is currently playing

○ **Uploading media**
qTweeter can upload locally stored media. Tapping on the photo/video icon will open up the gallery. Photos can be rotated before uploading

○ **Word counting**
For Twitter users the bottom left of the interface houses the obligatory character count. Very useful for staying inside those 140 character limits

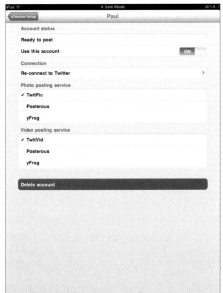

4: Final adjustments
Once qTweeter has connected to your Twitter account it will bring up a menu regarding your preferred media sharing outlets.

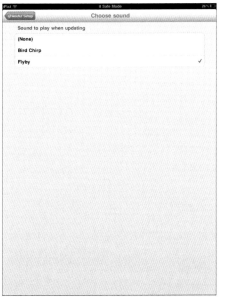

5: Audio alert
qTweeter includes a menu for selecting your Twitter alert. The Bird Chirp sound is the best Twitter chirp we've used yet.

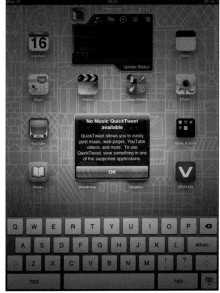

6: Application integration
qTweeter can instantly insert a tweet or Facebook update for you. It's also possible to post music, webpages and YouTube videos.

Control your iPad from your desktop machine

Just because your iPad is out of reach doesn't mean you can't use it…

App used: Veency **Price:** Free

Difficulty: Intermediate **Time needed:** 10-20 minutes

Veency is an app that allows your jailbroken iPad to be connected to your computer via a VNC connection. By using this tweak it's possible to view your iPad display and control everything that's on it from your computer. At first glance it's kind of difficult to imagine how having such a situation could garner any practical benefit, but with a little probing we managed to find some great reasons to use Veency.

For a start, Veency does a great job of mimicking the standard iPad gestures. Left clicking is like tapping the screen, while holding down the left button and moving the mouse is the equivalent of swiping across the display. Right-clicking replicates using the Home button and, if you have one, the middle button activates the lock/power switch on the top of the device.

You can also interact with any app that is waiting for a response. You can reply to that tweet, update that app and all without getting up from your chair. Even better, you can type messages using your own computer keyboard rather than the clunky alternative on the iPad display.

Veency | Set up a VNC connection

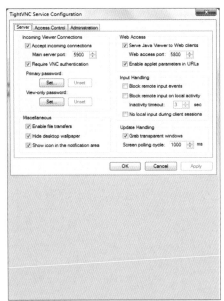

1: Head to Cydia
Veency is freely available on the Cydia network. Download the app and install it. You'll find it residing in the Settings menu.

2: Download VNC client
In order to connect your computer to your iPad you'll need to install a VNC client. In this example we're using TightVNC for Windows.

3: Address your IPs
Your VNC client needs to know your iPad's IP address to create a connection. Check it by pressing Settings>Wi-Fi>Network.

Tweaking Veency's settings

A quick glance at Veency's simplistic setup

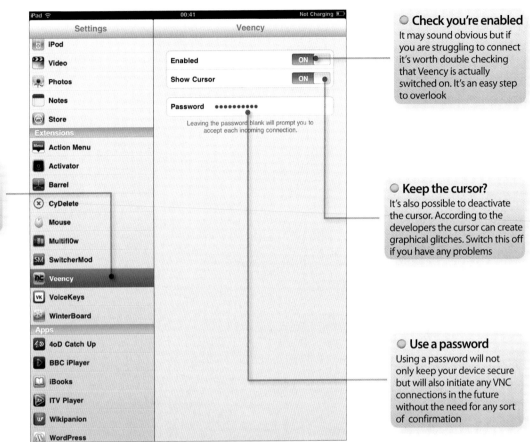

Check you're enabled
It may sound obvious but if you are struggling to connect it's worth double checking that Veency is actually switched on. It's an easy step to overlook

File under extensions
Veency doesn't have its own app icon; open the Settings menu and you'll find it tucked in the Extensions subsection

iPad Support Centre
As long as you don't have any problems with firewalls it's possible to log into other devices remotely. If you have a friend with a problematic jailbroken device you can log in via Veency and see first hand what the problem is.

Keep the cursor?
It's also possible to deactivate the cursor. According to the developers the cursor can create graphical glitches. Switch this off if you have any problems

Use a password
Using a password will not only keep your device secure but will also initiate any VNC connections in the future without the need for any sort of confirmation

4: Connect your iPad
Enter the IP address of your iPad into the VNC client on your computer. Click Connect to sync to your iPad.

5: Add a password
If everything is working properly your iPad will bring up a notification informing you that your computer is trying to connect.

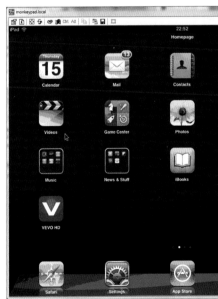

6: You're connected
Now you can control your iPad from your computer. To optimise the wireless stream we recommend using the 8-bit colour option.

iPad Tips, Tricks, Apps and Hacks **135**

Apps

The best apps that will help to extend the functionality of your iPad

Apps

The very best apps from the App Store that will help you do even more on your iPad

Apps

Price: £2.99/$5.99 **Developer:** Guinness World Records

Guinness World Records: At Your Fingertips

If you want to be a record breaker, this is what you need…

Spread across a handful of extreme categories (including Tallest, Craziest and Most Expensive), Guinness World Records: At Your Fingertips offers users an interesting insight into what it takes to become a legend among generations of drunks. This may occasionally require doing a little more than withstanding the pain of a needle or forgetting that falling causes death, but oh well.

Each category contains perhaps half a dozen or so separate entries chronicling various individuals' life work, making good use of the device's features through a range of interactive elements. These are often as simple as dots placed upon items of note that will bring up small portions of text thereon, but stretch to reveal a potential record attempt, no less. Using the constant connectivity of Apple's devices, the Guinness World Record for typing the alphabet backwards could very well be yours by the middle of next year. Sure, that hardly matches the 100 metres for prestige, but it's a start.

Aside perhaps from three-dimensional diagrams to manipulate, offering that additional level of presentational pizzazz, it's difficult to claim value for money isn't present here. Although the stuff covered is only a fraction of what you will find in the printed book, the way in which it is presented and the way in which you engage with it makes this feel like a whole new voyage of discovery. More bulk and even more innovation would be welcome in future editions but for now this a good, solid read.

■ There is loads to see and do on each page, make this a far more engaging prospect than the printed edition

■ With so much going on the size of the app is pretty large compared to most books

Rating ★★★★☆

SciFiNow Magazine

Price: £1.49/$1.99 **Developer:** Pixelmags

The world's leading science fiction magazine comes to the iPad

■ The content is presented exactly as per the magazine, you just swipe to turn pages

■ All the goodness of the magazine minus the hassle of finding a place to store all of your old copies

The debate as to whether the internet or a magazine is better is never going to die. Both boast positive and negatives that the other would love to include/exclude and it's unlikely one will ever ride out on top. What will, however, is a mix of both.

Giving you a free issue of the magazine when you purchase the app, SciFiNow opens up the ability to buy every back copy released and gives you instant access to the monthly publication as soon as it goes on-sale. Reading it on iPad is a treat. Flicking through the pages with your fingers or zooming into a particular article, which is heightened thanks to the iPad's slick resolution and speed, is effortless and makes the experience as good as having the actual print magazine. In some instances it's even easier as bookmarking a page or searching for a particular feature is as simple as a touch of a button. You can even share an issue with a friend who also has the app installed, making the app as close to its real-life counterpart as possible.

Rating ★★★★★

Stanza

Price: Free **Developer:** Lexcycle

It's a library, bookstore, text book and portable PDF reader all in one!

You may be wondering why you would need Stanza when iBooks comes free with the iPad. Well, while iBooks is a perfectly good eBook reader, albeit with overpriced books to download, Stanza offers so much more flexibility and customisation and a choice of online bookstores to visit. There are links in Stanza to more than 100,000 books, covering all subjects and genres. As they come from a variety of bookstores, there is competition on pricing, so costs are kept reasonable. Once you have downloaded a selection, you can view them in a cover flow style, giving the true bookshop feel to your experience as you flick through. That's not all, though; you can customise the font sizes and colours, read in portrait or landscape, adjust line spacing and there's a full-screen option so you can fully immerse yourself in a book.

What impressed us though was the ability to drop eBooks and PDF files onto a tab in iTunes and have these files pop-up to be read within Stanza. This means that you are no longer tied to only downloading on the iPad, and you can copy over your library of books from any PC or Mac.

Rating ★★★★☆

■ Have international best-sellers in your hands at the touch of a few buttons…

■ Text can be customised in many ways, adjusting colours, sizes and spacing to suit your preferences

Apps

Price: £2.99/$4.99 **Developer:** Gameloft SA

War In The Pacific
Immerse yourself in history

With shows like *The Pacific* and *Band Of Brothers* giving World War II's most prolific campaigns a lick of Hollywood gloss, it's no surprise to see historical texts receiving the same treatment. War In The Pacific is an engrossing history lesson for anyone looking to learn more about the Pacific Theatre. It's an app that will appeal even to those with an in-built aversion to reading books on the subject, thanks to the rousing orchestral soundtrack and the abundance of striking photography from the frontlines.

Throughout each of the 20 in-depth chapters, you will find well-documented first-hand accounts of each significant event throughout the campaign, surrounded by photos complete with captions, leaked documents from war officials and boxouts that elaborate on some of the more detailed elements. Page presentation is delivered in razor-sharp HD, and thanks to some neat menu design any user can flick through pages and jump to specific sections with ease. Chapters can be viewed in a simple playlist menu, or can be charted on an intricate map of the Pacific region to follow the flow of the greatest battles.

Rating ★★★★★

■ The bombastic score and poignant photography complement the book

Price: £0.69/$0.99 **Developer:** Pixelmags

Go Run Magazine
Thinking about running? This will help you every step of the way

We all pledge, often in an alcohol-induced haze on New Year's Eve, to rid our bodies of toxins and get fit for the forthcoming year. Granted, such resolutions are usually swiftly forgotten about, but if you're serious about improving your fitness then the Go Run app provides the perfect springboard for your ambitions.

This digital magazine is geared towards runners of all abilities, offering useful tips that can be read on the move and practical advice on training and nutrition. When you download the app you will get part one of 'The Beginner's Guide To Running', which is the first of many in-app books that will steadily help you enhance your running skills. In fact, the app pledges to help you train for your first 5K run from scratch in just 12 weeks!

The pages of this eBook are informative and eye-catching without bombarding you with text. Everything is kept waffle-free in bite-sized segments, providing only the essential information you need to get going, which is friendly and encouraging.

Rating ★★★★★

■ The app will get you ready for your first 5K

■ The app manages to be both educational and fun

Apps

Gems and Jewels
Price: £9.99/$13.99 **Developer:** Touch Press

Captivating visuals enhance this guide to precious stones

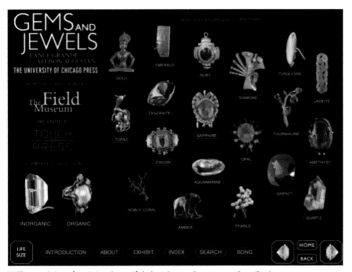

■ The app's interface is just beautiful; there's no other way to describe it

When the iPad was launched back in spring 2010, one of the apps that showcased it was a stunning interactive version of the periodic table called Elements, used because of the way it harnessed the iPad's capabilities and showed it off to be the show-stopping gadget it really is.

Gems and Jewels comes from the same developers, Touch Press, and works in a similar way, presenting a dazzling array of over 300 3D renditions of precious stones, shown in their naturally occurring states as well as jewelled settings, that can be spun, pinch-zoomed and generally messed with against a classy black background.

The download comes in at a jaw-dropping 1.66GB, so you know before you've even launched the app that it's a serious piece of work. Each item can be viewed from multiple angles and perspectives, and is accompanied by authoritative captions that tell you what you're looking at. A beautifully presented treasure trove of information, Gems and Jewels represents another perfect showcase for the iPad's capabilities.

Rating ★★★★★

Price: £9.99/$13.99 **Developer:** Touch Press

The Waste Land

A content-rich version of TS Eliot's greatest work

Hailed as one of the seminal works of poetry of the 20th Century, TS Eliot's *The Waste Land* is undeniably a complex work of great depth and vision. This app is a comprehensive collection of reference materials, interviews, video clips and audio readings that lifts the lid on many of the references and allusions found in the poem. It includes a specially filmed video performance by Fiona Shaw synced to the text, two readings by Eliot himself, other readings by Viggo Mortensen, Alec Guinness and Ted Hughes and over 35 video perspectives from respected contributors.

The app is beautifully produced and the light, airy interface style makes it a complete joy to use. A must for students of literature and poetry fans, this is a shining example of how today's technology can breathe new life into the classics.

Rating ★★★★★

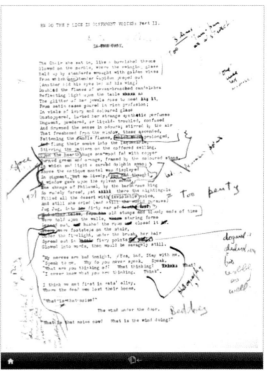

■ Includes full video performance by Fiona Shaw

Apps

Price: £11.99/$16.99 **Developer:** DataViz, Inc

Documents To Go Premium – Office Suite

View, manage and edit your documents on the move

Trawl through the App Store, and you'll come across a countless stack of apps that allow you to transport files and edit them on your iPad, but Documents To Go Premium is hands down the best of the bunch.

Admittedly, one glance at the price is enough to deter most casual app buyers, but if you require a means to bridge the gap between home and office, then this is perfect. The app works in tandem with a desktop app that you can download from the DataViz site, enabling you to drag documents into desktop folders, sync your desktop to your iPad, and then view and work on the same documents on your portable device. It is capable of syncing more than one desktop to the app, making it a convenient means of porting documents between home and work while using your commuting time to work on them.

The app supports Microsoft Word, Excel and PowerPoint files, and any changes you need to make can be applied to the iPad versions of the documents, saved, and then with a quick sync back to your desktop the amended and updated files will be transported back to where they originated from.

The effectiveness of Documents To Go Premium isn't confined to just synced folders either, as you can also view and manipulate supported attachments sent via the default Mail app, MS Exchange and Google Mail. Additionally, you can also pluck documents from a wide range of supported cloud storage devices – enabling you to work virtually whenever and wherever you see fit.

Despite such a seemingly relentless gush of positivity however, Documents To Go Premium isn't perfect. Conspicuous by its absence is a spell checker, and we did experience some slight syncing issues (the desktop and iPad just seemed to lose their connection to each other periodically), but certainly the latter problem seems to have been addressed with the 4.0.2 update. A simple and effective solution for your data transfer needs, Documents To Go Premium will undoubtedly help you work remotely.

■ After downloading the app, go to the DataViz website at **www.dataviz.com** and download the desktop app

Rating ★★★★★

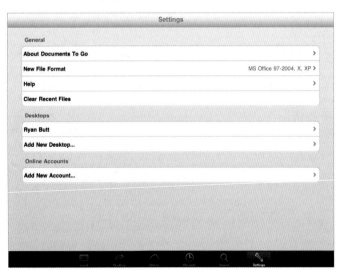

■ To get started, open up the app on your device, tap on the 'Settings' option at the bottom of the page and then tap 'Add'

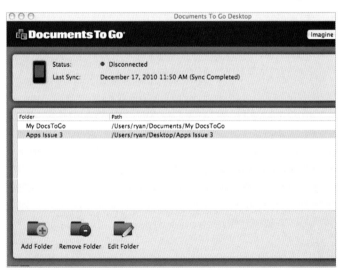

■ You can access the contents of your desktop folder through the app. If you make any changes then hit the 'Sync' button to update the changes on your computer

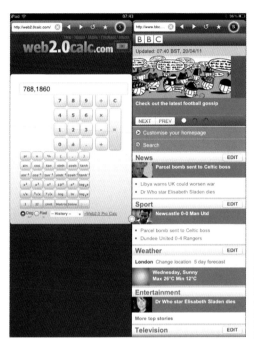

■ Users can switch a window to notes and copy and paste content from the opposite window

Price: £1.49/$1.19 **Developer:** BL

Side by Side Pro

Go multi-screen, and start multitasking while on the web

The iPad offers nearly ten inches of screen real estate. What is doesn't provide is the option to split up the screen to accommodate more than one window. However, this is exactly what Side by Side Pro does. The app is a multi-window reader/browser with offline reading and note-taking capabilities.

The split window scenario is nothing new to desktop users, but having the choice on the iPad is definitely a plus point. By default, the start page screen is split into two columns, with a host of links to the left and more in-depth info to the right. The first instinct is to tap an option on the left and see the right panel update. Obviously, this doesn't happen, as the windows operate independently. However, the side-by-side stance is still perfect for picking a topic left, and investigating further via the right.

Switching orientation from portrait to landscape also opens up the window content, making it easier to read. A button sits between the multiple screens, and a quick tap allows the user to resize a column to give it more – or less – screen space.

Rating ★★★★☆

Price: £2.99/$4.99 **Developer:** ITCreate

BluePrint Sketch

Sketch all of your bright ideas onto blueprint paper

We have to admit, there's something magical about blueprints. After all, the rockets that took mankind to the moon and back were designed on humble blueprint paper. Don't raise your hopes too high, however, as this is more of a sketching tool with the ability to create quick drawings and design layouts than an app to create a spaceship.

The intuitive interface makes it easy to manipulate objects. At the bottom of the screen is a tab bar with buttons for adding symbols, signatures and fonts; in total there are 36 objects to be used, which should be plenty. With just a tap of a finger, objects can be re-sized and edited. It's also possible to edit the fill colour and borders to give objects a unique appearance.

It's easy to whip up a sketch in mere seconds, but by digging further into the interface, more additional features appear. It's possible to group and copy objects, move them via a virtual control stick, and share them with friends via email. Sketches can also be saved to the iPad's gallery for later viewing. Great for brainstorming and object-based sketching, but not suitable for those looking to actually blueprint an idea.

Rating ★★★★☆

■ This app is great for sketching out any ideas that pop into your head, but its extensive features make it useful for a variety of purposes…

■ The interface allows you to quickly email sketches directly from the app

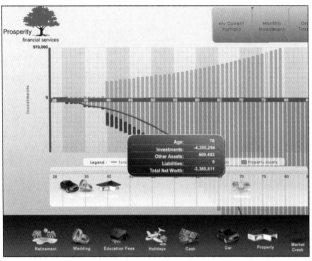

Wealth Manager
Price: £0.69/$0.99 **Developer:** Prosperity Financial Services PTE Ltd

Worried about the future? This might make things better, or worse…

There are a huge number of personal finance management apps available on the App Store, so it can be difficult for one to stand out from the crowd. And in these times of financial crisis, a lot of these apps are going to help a lot of people keep track of their cash, and will see plenty of people hoping that all the lines on the graph don't go too far down!

Wealth Manager is all about ensuring you can live to a ripe old age (assuming you do), with enough money to keep you going. And it does a fairly good job of this. It allows you to plot your age, how long you intend/expect to live, how much cash you're willing to put away per month, and exactly when you hope to retire. Sprinkle in extra cash vacuums like marriage, cars, holidays and homes, including exactly how expensive you'd like them to be, and the app will then produce a graph showing how long (or not) your cash is likely to last. It's all perfectly simple drag-and-drop stuff, with some easy to understand pop-up menus. And though there's no tutorial, we got to grips with it within minutes. Depressing affirmation of life's realities aside, it's really quite useful, and at this price it shouldn't affect your retirement fund too much.

■ Track your cash and see if you have enough to see you right

Rating ★★★★☆

AgileBoard

Price: £3.99/$5.99 **Developer:** Atlu Mantri

It's your own whiteboard, only smaller

The AgileBoard app replicates your own personal whiteboard. The app allows you to create columns of specific business, add notes, change their colour, and customise them according to your needs. It breaks down tasks into a manageable form, but requires that you have a very hands-on approach. Unfortunately, it doesn't act like a calendar, or 'talk' to your iPad's calendar, and won't remind you about timed events. You have to keep referring to it, which is perhaps the reason it allows you to screenshot your board for ease of access.

Simplicity is probably AgileBoard's greatest asset. While keeping track of your progress can lead to a mess of information in almost any other form (particularly written, our handwriting is terrible), AgileBoard keeps things tidy and clear.

Rating ★★★☆☆

"It breaks down tasks into a manageable form, but requires a hands-on approach"

■ It might look simple, but keeping things clear is the best way to use this app

Price: Free **Developer:** Willflow Limited

TED

Inspirational videos whenever you need them

While YouTube will forever be the place to indulge in all your video-related fantasies, TED offers a fine alternative. Based around a group of educational, inspirational and inspiring videos, this app allows you to search through TED's catalogue and watch talks and seminars from a range of different speakers for instant inspiration. There's a tremendous amount of content to be explored, and although a number of videos aren't as good as others, overall there's something for everyone, as long as it fits into one of the app's predetermined categories.

These set groupings are varied, though, incorporating everything from lectures on humour to culture. The search function also stretches this even further, with elements that may not be directly associated within a certain type still existing within the app. It has to be said that the download itself can be a little bit fiddly. It's far too easy to get stuck in a menu, and it can often take far too long before a video starts playing, but given the detailed information for each presenter and the quality of each video, this really is a tremendous app with plenty to offer in numerous areas.

Tailor-made for the iPad (and now available on iPhone and iPod touch), you have complete access to the full back-catalogue of TEDTalks

from some of the world's most fascinating people, including education radicals, tech geniuses, medical mavericks, business gurus and music legends. There are more than 900 videos to view (and more added each week) and these can be viewed in both high or low-res formats depending on your current network connectivity or stored to view offline later.

Options include the ability to curate your own playlist of inspiring speeches, share your favourites with friends and even tell the app how much viewing time you have available and it will hand-pick some videos to suit your needs. You can even stream the videos onto the big screen via AirPlay – which is handy for the boardroom or the classroom when attempting to inspire young and impressionable minds.

There's even a subtitled version offered by TED, meaning that regardless of what your situation may be, this is an app you should – at the very least – try out. A huge database of inspirational, information and humorous videos, TED makes you realise just how good the App Store is. As a free download, you really have nothing to lose by downloading it, but everything to gain.

Rating ★★★★☆

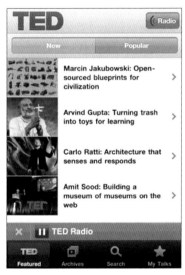

■ You can jump straight to the most popular videos or search for something specific…

■ The app draws on an impressive database of speakers from the very pinnacle of their respective professions…

Price: Free **Developer:** NASA Ames Research Center

NASA App HD

A free app from NASA that's out of this world

This official app from NASA offers users an almost overwhelming amount of content for nothing and covers everything from space and the universe to NASA and its various missions.

Launch the app and you'll be greeted by the NASA Launch Schedule and an A-Z list of current NASA missions. The layout on the main screen is similar to the iPhone's Contacts app, making it incredibly easy to navigate. Everything from the Hubble Space Telescope to the International Space Station is listed and clicking on an entry will give you more details about it.

Each listing comes with an introduction and facts about the mission, with one of the coolest features being the ability to check the current location and path of missions via Google Maps. There are also gorgeous images of space taken from the missions and videos and interviews from the excellent NASA TV, while there are pleasingly regular news updates and you can even find out how long missions have been in orbit for. It really does give a remarkable insight into the workings of NASA and its various missions throughout the years.

It would be wrong to keep your newfound knowledge to yourself so sharing it has been made very simple and can be done through Facebook and Twitter or via email. For a free app, the amount of content on offer here is incredible, so much so that we would almost be happy

to pay for it. Whether you're interested in NASA's projects yourself or you have a child or sibling who is learning about space exploration then this is a brilliant learning tool that provides great insight into the missions past and present. It is also packed with great special effects – such as launch information and countdown clocks that really engage the user.

A great app packed full of valuable information, there is no reason not to download this immediately and enjoy an entire universe of information at your fingertips – regular updates keep things running smoothly too.

Rating ★★★★★

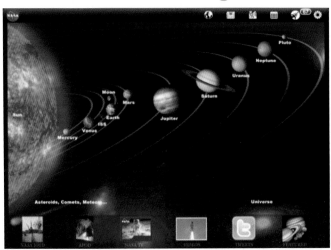

■ The app is packed full of information from NASA's proud history of space travel

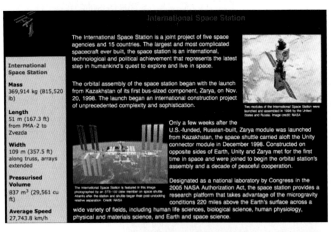

■ One of the best features is the ability to check mission paths via Google Maps

Price: Free **Developer:** ComiXology

Comics

Enjoy classic comics on the move

Anyone who's spent time with the Marvel or DC Comics apps will feel right at home with ComiXology's Comics app. It's exactly the same technology except that it features comics from all kinds of publishers, along with ones from the big two mentioned before.

The app features a very slick and user-friendly interface that is easy to navigate and never buries any of its content out of sight. Just like the aforementioned apps, its best features are that it has a section dedicated to free comics, which is updated regularly and it uses 'Guided View Technology' to make the reading experience as pleasant as possible on the small screen. Intelligently panning and zooming around the comic page, it's a great solution to the problem of small-screen viewing.

The only slight niggle was that the app was occasionally prone to unexpected crashes, although we suspect that this was just a minor glitch that has since been eradicated by an update. A polished product for comic fans everywhere, this makes reading comics on the move a real pleasure. Highly recommended to everyone.

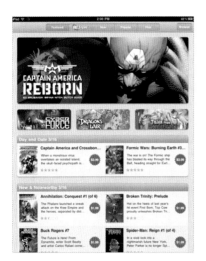

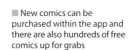

■ New comics can be purchased within the app and there are also hundreds of free comics up for grabs

Rating ★★★★☆

Price: Free **Developer:** VEVO LLC

VEVO HD

Music videos come alive on iPad

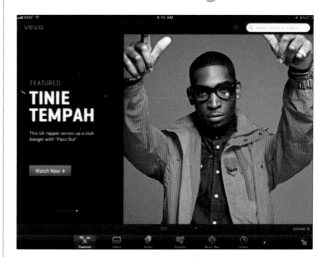

VEVO is an online entertainment platform dedicated to bringing you the latest music videos. Directed at music lovers, the quality and variety of videos is something to boast about. With over 25,000 videos from 7,500 artists, there is plenty of choice on offer.

You can browse the feature section, search for artists, or filter your search. This is all standard, but VEVO also lets you know if that artist is on tour, allows you to buy gig tickets and purchase songs. You can also share videos on social networking sites, bring up info about the artist, view their Twitter feed and more.

The videos vary from live performances, interviews and music videos. The introductions to each video are annoying, but it disguises the loading time, so this is not too much of a problem. The ability to leave comments or ratings would be nice, but all in all this is a comprehensive app that could provide music fans with that little bit beyond what you get with similar established apps.

VEVO HD is an excellent app that is packed with a variety of useful options and features a wide range of artists to suite all tastes. Unfortunately it's just lacking user interactivity.

Rating ★★★★☆

■ VEVO brings you easy access to gig tickets for your favourite artists

■ Choose from a wide variety of videos from over 7,500 artists

Price: Free **Developer:** TapMedia Ltd

Tap TV

Watch classic movies and cartoons plus the best of YouTube

There are many different ways you can watch video on the iPad, but the truth is that videos are only as good as the source they come from. What Tap TV offers is the ability to 'tap' into an extensive archive of videos to watch via Wi-Fi at any time you see fit. As you might expect, the app is split into a diverse range of channels: movies, cartoons, documentaries, App TV, audiobooks, Magic TV, Best of YouTube and Silent Classics. Unfortunately, when it comes to movies or cartoons you're unlikely to find anything particularly new, but it's a great source of ancient classics that you can educate or just plain torture your kids with, or watch on your own for pure nostalgia value (and the inevitable swell of mild disappointment that accompanies returning to your childhood favourites).

We found some excellent old Warner Bros cartoons lurking in the lists, and some great Charlie Chaplin movies that you probably won't have seen for years! There are new videos too though, particularly on the documentaries and App TV channels.

The app is well laid out with easy-to-navigate menus, the only downside is that some videos are a little slow to load.

■ The interface is attractive enough

Rating ★★★★☆

Price: Free **Developer:** Fabien Sanglard

Fluid

Turn your iPad into your personal pool

Fluid does nothing more than turn your iPad into a pool of rippling water. It sounds pointless and in a way it is, but there's something compelling about Fabien Sanglard's app and we'd be lying if we didn't admit to wasting a good hour of our time messing around with Fluid when we first discovered it.

The concept is simplicity in itself. There is no game, no real point to it; you simply drag your fingers across the water's surface in order to manipulate it. And yet despite this Fluid is actually a lot of fun and surprisingly absorbing, simply because the physics for it are so good. It's utterly mesmerising to watch the swirling patterns as you drag your fingers through the water, and even though there's not really a lot to it, you'll still discover it to be an entertaining time-waster.

A slider adjusts the speed of the water, there's the option to turn the soothing background music off and it's even possible to import your own images to use as your pool's base (which is more than a little disconcerting if you've chosen a photo of a loved one). Yes this app is little more than a tech demo, but Fluid remains an impressive one.

Rating ★★★☆☆

■ The app is fairly pointless, but it can be a great tool to relieving stress as you swish the water

■ You can import photos into the app and then move them around as if they were made of water

"It's mesmerising to watch the swirling patterns"

Price: £2.99/$4.99 **Developer:** Gameloft

Fast Five

Fast, furious and packed full of high-octane mayhem

Drawing heavily from the mechanics of its *Asphalt* racing games, Gameloft's *Fast Five* is a hefty title that delivers more content than its small asking price suggests. It follows ex-FBI agent Brian O'Conner – played by Paul Walker in the Hollywood movie – as he pulls off a seemingly small heist, and unknowingly triggers a larger, more deadly chain of events that leads him and his crew to Rio de Janeiro.

Fast Five is purely a racing game, so all of the on-foot action and shooting from the movies are nowhere to be seen, and only mentioned in mid-chapter conversations between O'Conner and other characters. On-foot shooting sections would have certainly mixed up each chapter, as they are essentially all just a string of similar race types that quickly become a tad too familiar after only a few events.

You can unleash a nitro burst by tapping the icon on the left for a speed boost, or to give yourself more ramming power for taking out other drivers. Rewind power-ups can also be used up to three times in most races, letting you undo misjudged turns or devastating crashes. The rewind skill is helpful given how perilous some tracks can be.

Drifting, however, isn't. Tapping the brake lightly while turning is supposed to result in a drift that rewards you with bonus cash at the end of each race. However, it tightens your turning arc so severely that cornering effectively becomes a real pain. Drift events that demand you slide round bends as often as you can quickly become an irritating slog as a result, and may have you reaching for the quit icon fast.

The Underground Market menu lets you select one of many race modifiers that can give an advantage on the tarmac, such as bursting the tyres of another racer, swapping around grid positions before the start of a race, and more. Some of these are big gambles, but when they pay off, they pay off big.

You can also spend your winnings on new cars, or tune up your existing rides, as well as modify the appearance of any vehicle with new body kits. Money and experience can be either won or bought with actual money via the in-game storefront, but progressing through using this method waters down the replay value somewhat.

Fast Five is a huge game at a modest asking price, and while the controls may feel slack and erratic at the outset, practising to get a feel for the tilt sensitivity is to be advised. That aside, this is another solid racing title from Gameloft.

Rating ★★★★☆

"Fast Five is a huge game at a rather modest asking price"

■ The graphical filters are cool, and aren't something that you'd expect in a game at this price point

Couldn't tell ya. But two of 'em went down when the shooting started. That ain't good.

Continue

■ The story's kind of nonsense, but what else would you expect from a *Fast Five* game?

Price: £1.99/$1.99 **Developer:** Minoraxis Inc

Fruit Juice Tycoon 2

Enron looks positively saintly by comparison

We've never set up a lemonade stall, but we imagine it to be a harmless, character-building and endearing experience. Not so in *Fruit Juice Tycoon 2*. Here, the juice industry is defined by hostile takeovers, political backstabbings, dirty tricks and even kidnapping. Don't let the bright colours fool you – we're surprised the corner stalls aren't ran by gangs.

It's the RPG elements that set this sequel apart, seeing you purchase stock, manage stalls and level up. For the most part, it plays as a business simulation/time management sim as you attempt to expand your business into new neighbourhoods, but the actual juice-selling part takes the form of a match-three game that's so simple you won't have any trouble satisfying customers.

The business and micromanagement aspect can actually feel quite involving, but it's the simplicity and repetitiveness of these more 'gamey' elements that let it down.

■ The gameplay is disappointing compared to the business side

Rating ★★★☆☆

"The business and micromanagement aspect can feel quite involving"

Price: £4.99/$0.99 **Developer:** Electronic Arts

NBA Jam by EA Sports

Still slamming strong after all these years

Back before phones barely had the technology to manage a call, and mobile gaming meant getting a bus to the nearest arcade, an unusual sports title was quickly becoming a smash hit. *NBA Jam* brought something new with its fast-paced action, over-the-top manoeuvres and hilarious commentator.

Now on the iPad, the new version seeks to relive that charm with the same mix of caricaturised players and frenetic action. And it does, in every possible way.

There are a number of abilities available. For example, block is used with a tap of the left button, yet hold down the central run button and swipe left, and your player will push their opponents. While this can be cumbersome at first, the controls eventually become second nature.

With 36 matches in each division, not to mention unlockable characters, basketballs and special modes, there's plenty here. *NBA Jam* manages to bring the playability and joy of the original into a neat and stylish package. A must-have game for your iPad, whether you're old enough to remember the original or not.

Rating ★★★★★

"The controls eventually become second nature"

■ Fans will be pleased to see the customary *NBA Jam* big heads are here in full force

 Although its graphics are insane, the controls deserve equal acclaim

You will probably face the God King many times!

Price: £3.99/$5.99 **Developer:** Chair Entertainment

Infinity Blade

So much more than a pretty face

Infinity Blade by Chair Entertainment – under the watchful eye of Epic Games – is the latest developer to jump onboard the iPad, and the end result is one of the best-looking iPad games ever.

Visuals are only half the story, however, as Chair has created a title which is just perfect for playing on the go. Taking control of a Knight, your goal is to defeat the God King, an impossible task that will see you die on your first attempt, only to take on the role of your child, eager to avenge the family bloodline.

Infinity Blade is all about repetition. You face the same enemy, walk through the same parts of the castle and will eventually die by the God King's hand until you finally develop the skills to defeat him. And yet for all its repetition and grinding gameplay, it's never boring to play.

This in part is due to the control system that has you parrying sword swipes and dodging and blocking blows with simple swipes and taps of your finger. It's a delightfully elegant control system that still requires a large amount of skill due to the different enemies that you face. Truly stunning stuff.

Rating ★★★★★

Price: £3.99/$6.99 **Developer:** Electronic Arts Inc

Tiger Woods PGA Tour 12 For iPad

Not quite a hole in one

This is more of an update than a sequel to previous games, although in fairness it doesn't deviate especially far from the controls of its predecessors.

The touch-screen swing mechanic returns, requiring the player to draw their finger down a meter and swipe to swing. You can draw and fade the ball by curving your finger's movement, and add spin by swiping during its trajectory.

The bulk of the play takes place in the PGA Tour, which sees you compete for cash prizes, which can then be used to enter tournaments or buy equipment. Smaller modes come in the form of the Tiger Challenge and Closest To The Pin. The latter mode is self-explanatory, but EA's decision to limit this multiplayer mode just to Facebook is odd.

The disappointing multiplayer decisions don't actually end there. While multiplayer is included, it's confined to Bluetooth and Wi-Fi, which is a shame as online play would have made the app a much more tempting proposition.

Rating ★★★★★

While there are better-looking sports games out there, the visuals can hold their own

The familiar Tiger controls are back – if it ain't broke and all that

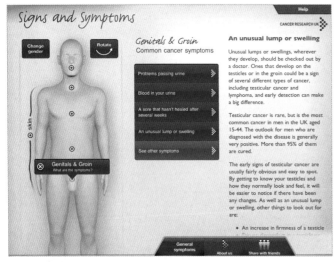

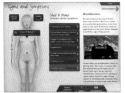 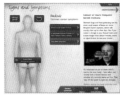

Some symptoms have videos to watch to illustrate the importance of getting a check up

Price: Free **Developer:** Cancer Research UK

Cancer Signs And Symptoms for iPad

Catch the signs of cancer early

 Cancer is a concern for everybody, and when you consider that many of us will contract it at some point in our lives, it pays to be vigilant and take notice of the warning signs that your body throws out.

How do you distinguish what could be something very innocent from a more serious symptom, though? This free app from Cancer Research UK is very simple to use. Simply select your gender and tap on one of the red hotspots that you're concerned about on the illustrated human. If, for example, you click on the breast area, you're presented with a list of common cancer symptoms. These categories are then explained in a little more detail, sometimes with video from sufferers and doctors with encouraging words.

What is good about this app is that it won't make you feel that every little lump, bump or cough could be a sign of a dreadful illness. Instead it holds your hand and encourages you to see a doctor without making you feel like you're wasting anyone's time. It doesn't cover every type of cancer, but just being aware of possible symptoms could save your life.

Rating ★★★★★

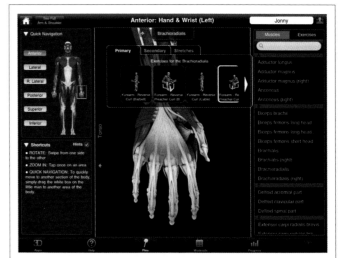

The app provides a detailed breakdown of each exercise and its potential benefits, making it easy to pick ones that are right for you

Price: £2.99/$4.99 **Developer:** 3D4Medical.com

iMuscle – (NOVA Series) – iPad Edition

In-depth exercises for every bit of your body

 iMuscle is an exercise app that – through the use of a 3D rendered human body – allows you to choose which areas of your body you want to exercise and how. The amount of information and exercises on offer is excellent. You can pretty much pick any muscle in the body, and be given a range of exercises.

With each exercise comes an animation showing you what to do, and plenty of information on how to do it. To take it all one step further, you can track your progress and manage workouts, adding specific exercises to a particular workout you want to do, and see what effect it's having on your body.

Our only problem is that the amount of information on offer can seem overwhelming at times, and those less in the know might be unsure of the benefits between two similar exercises, Recommended for fitness fanatics.

Rating ★★★★☆

Price: £1.99/$2.99 **Developer:** fraga games Ltd

Ming's Memory

Release your stress with a matching ball game

At first glance this looks like it should be in the game category of the App Store. However, once you've been immersed in Ming's Memory's world for a while, you'll begin to notice that you feel more relaxed. The soothing tunes and subtle backgrounds almost entice you into a meditative state, and

you can feel the stresses from the day flow from your body.

Like all the best stress relievers, the premise is very simple: match pairs of the floating yin/yang balls that are constantly moving. If you use it on the commute home from work we guarantee that you will start your evening in a better frame of mind.

■ Calming backgrounds and sounds help to soothe

Rating ★★★★☆

Price: £1.49/$1.99 **Developer:** Dee Zee

Healthy Tips For A Healthy Lifestyle

A healthy body means a healthy mind

Let's face it, we could all do with being a bit healthier. We know what we need to do to keep our bodies and minds healthy, but staying power is where we let ourselves down. However, this app will arm you with more information and some tips that can be incorporated into

your life. Discover how to increase your metabolism, how to eat good meals, and how a break from your desk each day will help keep your heart healthy.

■ Share your favourite tips via Facebook

Rating ★★★★☆

Price: £1.49/$1.99 **Developer:** ololac Interactive

eFitness Shoulder Workout

Learn more about the tops of your arms

The shoulder is an often-neglected part of the body. We tend to concentrate on having firm thighs, a flat stomach and eliminating those bingo wings; however, looking after your shoulders is – according

to this app – very important. And when you think about it, they do go through a lot each day, from lifting up the kids to carrying shopping. Here you can learn how to improve the joint flexibility and tone the areas around them for added strength.

■ Workout routines are set for all levels

Rating ★★★☆☆

Price: £2.99/$5.99 **Developer:** JX Mobile LLC

Pilates for iPad

Exercise techniques from an expert

Although the fitness and body toning technique of Pilates have been around since it was developed in Germany in 1880, it's only over the last decade that it has become popular. As it's one of the most popular classes at gyms and village halls, getting into a class that suits your timetable can be quite tricky. So this app which features exclusive movies that have been narrated and performed by an instructor is perfect as you can practise

the technique whenever you have your iPad in a spot with a Wi-Fi connection.

■ Follow the step-by-step instructions for each move

Rating ★★★★☆

Price: £1.99/$2.99 **Developer:** Omaxmedia

Maxjournal

This app lets you transform your iPad into an elegant daily journal

 Diary apps tend to fall into two categories – there's the personal assistant style of app that organises your appointments and schedules. Then there's the more relaxed type, based around the kind of journal in which some of us like to record the ins and outs of our day at its close, preferably with a nice hot drink and a curled-up pet snoozing somewhere nearby.

Maxjournal definitely falls into this second category, the design revolving around a virtual large-format journal of the type that can be found in expensive stationery shops. This instantly imbues it with an air of quality, oozing the sort of luxurious finger-appeal which makes it a pleasure to use.

The main interface consists of a large central page area with a dateline across the top which is also used for accessing the year and the month. Accompanying this is a set of small tabs down the left-hand side, each of which bears a date. When tapped, each tab brings up a whole page that corresponds to that day, ready to be filled with your thoughts and accounts of your exploits.

A cluster of buttons found on the upper right of the screen handles features such as: the comprehensive Export and Backup options, a search feature that can target specific words within your entries, the online help system and the font. Also handy is password protection setting where you can protect your thoughts from a nosey family. Photos and tags can be added, scrapbook style, in a panel on the right of the screen, and a large 'Today' button rounds things off, allowing you to zip right to the current day's page with a single touch.

Tap a page and it zooms instantly to fill the iPad's screen, tap once more and up pops the keyboard ready to make an entry. There is a choice of 16 different fonts of variable sizes, old favourites such as Helvetica and Marker Felt Wide being joined by more esoteric choices like Journal and Kayleigh, which lend a more handwritten feel to jottings.

Other than changing the size and font however, there seem to be no other text style formatting options available, a shame as it would be nice to be able to use Bold and Italic styles for extra expressive entries. Overall, Maxjournal is one of the best of this type of app that we've seen and it should definitely be considered at the relatively low price.

■ The main interface is uncluttered and efficient, getting you to your entries quickly

Rating ★★★★★

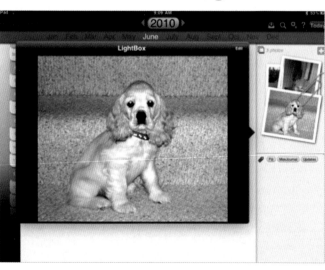

■ Excellent export and backup options include a variable date range

■ Each entry in your journal can be accompanied by up to three photos…

Price: Free **Developer:** Yell Ltd

Yell.com

Why shout for help when you can Yell?

Forget calling all those ridiculous premium rate numbers and just use this all-in-one, all-round awesome app when you need to find what you need to find. Want to locate the nearest supermarket? No problem. Fancy a pizza? Crack out the tomato sauce. Stuck in a new place with no way home? Find the nearest taxi firm with a touch of a screen and flick of a finger.

The Yell.com app presents you with a search bar or a list of areas such as restaurants, cinemas and hotels for you to choose from. Using your current location, it finds the nearest results for your request and presents you with either a list including the distance, address and phone number or a map view of where they all are. You can add the number straight to your contact book or to your favourites, share it on Facebook, Twitter or by email and even call direct from the app. The map can be presented in satellite view as well and it will also plot a route for you.

Yell.com was quick to load, and at no cost, it's a fantastic addition to your essential app line-up. It seems that, in our digital age, the old-fashioned Yellow Pages directories can now be relegated to doorstops, as this has all the info on local businesses you need.

Rating ★★★★★

"It's a fantastic addition to your essential app line-up"

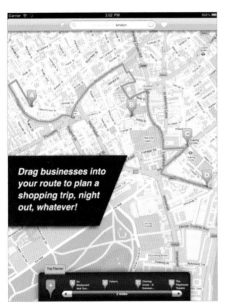

Drag businesses into your route to plan a shopping trip, night out, whatever!

All the information you need, at your fingertips

■ The app contains all of the information on local businesses that you could ever need

■ Handy maps show you exactly where you need to go

■ Each pack comes with a stack of 60 questions

■ This app is a good ice-breaker for get-togethers…

Price: £1.99/$3.99 **Developer:** Aloompa

Tabletopics HD

How exactly can conversations be more interactive?

Tabletopics – originally a card game to be played with friends – seeks to make conversations 'better' and 'more interactive'. Now it's been ported over to the iPad, bringing the card game from the dining room to the coffee table.

With the initial purchase, you'll have two packs – Starter Set and Happy Hour – each with a collection of 60 themed questions, intended to provoke interesting, entertaining and/or enlightening answers for you and your friends. There are no rules, and there is no failure; simply one question after another. How you decide to handle these questions is up to you.

Each pack can be played in two ways: either by picking a card from the top, or choosing from six overturned cards. Alongside this is the option to hide unwanted questions so they won't appear, or mark favourites from the collection, including saving the most memorable responses.

Tabletopics HD does its job just fine. But the price isn't worth what is essentially a handful of questions. However, it is a great idea for those who like a good get-together.

Rating ★★★☆☆

djay
Price: £13.99/$19.99 **Developer:** algoriddim

Is this music-mixing app Grandmaster Flash or flash in the pan?

Could the iPad be the next DJ turntable? With algoriddim's djay app, it's certainly an authentic-looking alternative. Its striking turntable/cross-fader interface reacts convincingly to touch input, but is it enough to substitute the unmistakable feel of working with 12" vinyl records? Perhaps not, but the cost and convenience of an iPad-based DJ set-up certainly has a number of distinct advantages.

Getting started is a breeze; simply open the app, and select a non-DRM track from your iTunes library. The djay app will then carefully calculate its tempo (or BPM – Beats Per Minute), draw a waveform of the track, and apply any available artwork to the record on the turntable. From choosing a track until it's ready to play, the whole process takes about 15 seconds.

The interface is reasonably intuitive, and within ten minutes of use it's possible for an experienced DJ to sound like they're performing on traditional DJ equipment. Novice DJs are also catered for within the app, with BPM sync tools that assist with mixing. Annoyingly, the BPM calculations can occasionally go awry, and we could find no way of manually correcting it. Whatever your skill level, djay also includes some fun and easy-to-learn scratching tricks that could otherwise take years to perfect on traditional DJ equipment.

Sadly, the Automix function doesn't always automatically 'beat-match' your tunes. Results seem to vary from one record to the next, making it

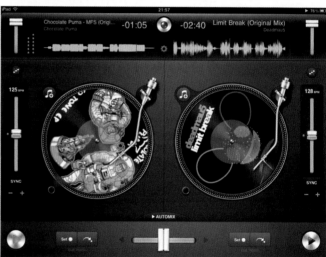

■ Getting started is a breeze, simply open the app and select a track from your iTunes library. You can then experiment and get accustomed to the set-up

possibly more suited for background music purposes. AirPlay support is included, but our attempts to wirelessly broadcast music created a latency that made beat-mixing records incredibly difficult. You can also record your masterpieces within the app and have it saved in AIFF format. Recordings can be exported via iTunes, or played back within the app itself.

Arguably, djay may lack the prestige of owning a proper turntable set-up, but it remains an accessible option for any wannabe DJ. Alternatively, experienced scratch DJs, or those accustomed to feature-packed 'CD Turntables' may find djay slightly lacking in advanced tools. Ultimately, it is best suited for enjoying at home, or for adding some excitement to a party. Intuitive, accessible and fun, djay is a solid turntable app.

> "From choosing a track until it's ready to play, the process takes 15 seconds"

Rating ★★★★☆

Price: £6.99/$9.99 Developer: Reactable Systems

Reactable Mobile

Getting to grips with the coolest synthesiser on iPad

Best described as a bizarre, futuristic synthesiser, the Reactable is a circular table, backlit with a deep blue light, to be used in a darkened room. The table itself is a touch-sensitive computer display that reacts to objects, called tangibles, that are placed on the screen, moved around and rotated. This creates different sorts of music depending on the type of tangibles that are placed on the table, their spatial relationship to one another and the way in which they are manipulated.

It's a very cool, almost sci-fi idea, and one that has been used by a number of high-profile performers including Björk. Sadly, at a price of around £8,500, the Reactable is far out of the reach of your average bedroom DJ, which is where the Reactable Mobile app comes in…

At a mere £6.99, Reactable Mobile is much more affordable than its rather expensive tabletop counterpart, and it does a pretty good impression of it too. Just like the original, it allows you to place various synthesiser functions onto the surface and play around with them to create your own music in real-time. The large iPad screen also works really well with it. When laid down flat on a table or other surface, we

felt like we were getting a fair approximation of the original technology, especially with the room to use both hands freely.

There's a truly mind-boggling array of options at your fingertips with Reactable Mobile – loop players, oscillators, wave shapers, sequencers and all number of other things we don't really understand but are sure will be most welcome with the musically inclined, especially as the software allows you to incorporate your own samples into the mix.

As amateurs with a distinct lack of any kind of electronic or acoustic musical talent, we had a lot of fun when simply experimenting with Reactable's 'tangibles' and were surprised by the music we were able to create, suggesting that those who know what they're doing will be able to produce absolutely exceptional results.

Just about the only fault we encountered was that the software struggled to keep up when we overloaded it with too many tangibles at once, but that may not be such big a deal. After all, how many bands do you see use more than a handful of instruments at once? Reactable Mobile is an overwhelmingly complex music app that's sure to strike the right note with those who 'get it'.

"Reactable Mobile is much more affordable than its tabletop counterpart"

■ The app is a bargain compared to the tabletop version

Rating ★★★★☆

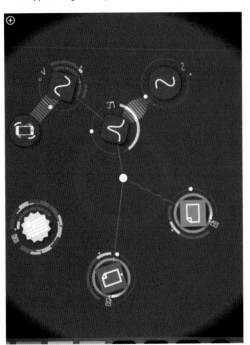

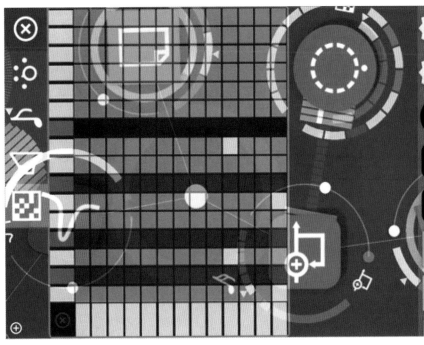

Price: £2.99/$4.99 Developer: Marco Arment

Instapaper Pro

Save what you're reading and catch up later

I Instapaper Pro is an incredibly handy app that enables you to save whatever you're currently viewing so that you can read it at a later date.

Once you've registered the app – something that you will have to do – you'll gain access to plenty of useful features that make using this app an absolute breeze. Due to the way apps are set up, you'll need to make a few physical adjustments in order to add Instapaper to Safari, but the instructions are straightforward and a lot easier to use than other apps of this type. It's also compatible with Tumblr and Twitter, which is very handy indeed.

After everything is set up, it's simply a case of looking through your favourite sites and choosing what you want to read. Simply select a page, go to your bookmarks, hit 'Instapaper: Read Later' and it will immediately save your page. Anything you select is instantly saved to folders in the Instapaper app, ready for you to view when you actually have the time.

It should be worth noting that the saved pages are very basic – getting rid of most of the available pictures and ads that were on the previous version – but you're left with just the text which is nice and easy to read and something that Apple has incorporated into Safari as standard with the recent iOS 5 update. If reading is an issue you can change the font and size and even switch between light and dark text. You can even enable a tilt mode to scroll through articles if you're too lazy to do it yourself.

While the free version of Instapaper is more than adequate for most of your daily needs, there's no denying that the additional features included in Instapaper Pro are worth it.

Extremely easy to set up and very user-friendly, Instapaper Pro is an excellent app that ensures that you'll always find the time to look at everything you need to, regardless of whether or not you currently have access to Wi-Fi. We're not sure how the developer will evolve the app so that it is still appealing to the masses and useful after Apple's aforementioned software update, but for now it is undoubtedly the best app of its kind.

With some very useful features, Instapaper Pro is the perfect way of reading the web in your own time, minus all of the clutter and adverts that you usually have to navigate your way through to read the bare bones of the pages and stories that interest you. Download it now and you'll be surprised how quickly it becomes integrated into your daily webpage-reading routine.

Rating ★★★★☆

■ You can save pages to read later, minus all of the pictures and clutter

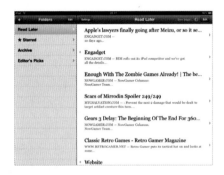

■ The app is integrated into Safari and is accessible from the 'Bookmarks' button

"It is the perfect way of reading the web in your own time"

■ The look and feel of the app is quite sterile but it definitely serves its purpose

■ The app includes two different font sizes to ensure that it is easy to read…

Price: Free **Developer:** Evening Standard

Evening Standard for iPad

All the latest news in an easy-to-read format

If you live in London or the South West area then you'll find this app to be highly informative. While the iPhone version is rather cluttered, it truly shines on the larger iPad screen thanks to good design and layout and very easy-to-read text. There are five separate categories to choose from: News, Business, Sports, Showbiz, and Life and Style, as well as the option to look at any previous stories that you have saved. Video is also included, although we were unable to view anything as the pad stated it wasn't enabled for HTML5 delivery.

When held in landscape mode all the latest stories are displayed down the far-left side of the screen, and it's a relatively simple task to scroll through for any older stories. Topics of interest can be mailed or linked to Twitter and Facebook and there are two different font sizes that make for an easier reading experience.

While there are ads on every page, they aren't too intrusive and it's difficult to complain when you're getting regular information for absolutely nothing. It is fairly sterile in its look and design, but as a quick, easy-to-use news source it's still highly useful.

Rating ★★★★☆

"Topics of interest can be mailed or linked to Twitter and Facebook"

Price: Free **Developer:** AOL

Engadget for iPad

Essential technology news

Upon loading the app you can tap into four channels: Engadget, iMobile, Engadget HD and alt.Engadget, and all serve up a rich feast of regularly updated news stories, plus photo galleries and video feeds. The screen is efficiently presented with scrollable stories across a top bar, and news previews in the main window that you can tap on to be taken through to the full story and accompanying links. What's more, a handy side-tab allows you to post comments on any of the stories, and a side-column on the front page displays the most-commented stories, so you can instantly jump to what everyone's talking about.

The app is completed by launch pads along the bottom of the screen that take you to photo and video galleries, saved stories, hot topics and news archives. But the real icing on the cake is the 'Podcasts' tab that lets you listen to Engadget's latest audio feeds within the app itself. Whether you have an enthusiastic interest in technology or simply want to gaze at how a great news app should be done, Engadget is a must-download app that is a joy to behold. One of the best news apps available for the iPad that deserves to be digested.

Rating ★★★★★

■ A timeline is regularly updated with all the latest happenings…

■ The app draws content from a rich list of sites so that you always stay informed

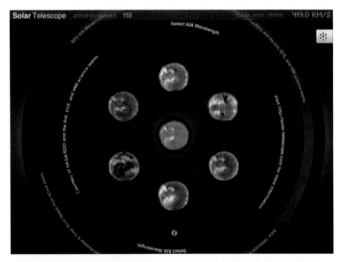

■ Zoom in close to check out flares

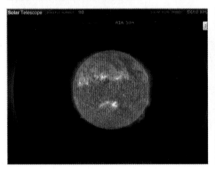 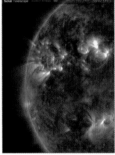

Price: £1.49/$1.99 **Developer:** egrafic

Solar Telescope HD

Monitor solar activity on your iPad screen

 "Don't look at the Sun, you'll hurt your eyes!" If this sentence is still fresh in your memory from childhood, then egrafic's Solar Telescope HD will provoke a small smile of satisfaction. It allows you to view regularly updated, high-resolution images of the Sun in seven different AIA wavelengths (or 'colours' as we call them here on Earth) taken by NASA's dedicated sungazing SDO (Solar Dynamics Observatory) spacecraft.

The shots are very impressive, revealing the apparently benign yellow ball in our sky to be what appears to be a raging, angry fiery giant. The app's interface is brilliantly sci-fi, actually making you feel like you're using a real telescope, and the navigation is intuitive, allowing you to zoom in close and pan around the images by double-tapping and finger-scrolling. Plenty of information is provided, with the date and time that each image was taken, the sunspot number in the frame and the real-time solar wind speed.

Rating ★★★★☆

■ The minimal design is very easy on the eye

■ Choose one of 12 different themes…

Price: £1.49/$1.99 **Developer:** Bigsool

Weather Station World

Transform your iPad into a global weather station

If you've ever lusted after one of those digital weather centres that you used to see in the Innovations catalogue, now's your chance. Weather Station World turns your iPad into a £500 version of that very device. The app's clear, uncluttered layout and minimalistic design really does look fabulous on the crisp iPad display, particularly in the dark, and it displays a wealth of weather-related information, including the time and date, current temperature and barometric pressure, five-day forecast, humidity, wind speed and direction, dewpoint, probability of rain and sunrise and sunset times. A selection of 12 different colour schemes are available too, so you should have no problem finding one that suits your mood. You can easily set a new location by dropping a pin onto a global Google map, which can then be saved to a favourites list for easy retrieval later on. A great-looking app that's great to use.

Rating ★★★★★

"A selection of 12 colour schemes are available"

Price: £1.49/$1.99 **Developer:** Global Delight Technologies

Photo Delight Hand-paint some colour into your pics with this cool app

Although there are a number of apps with similar functions available within the App Store, Photo Delight nevertheless manages to score highly thanks to its ease of use, smart tools and great options.

The reasons for this success are numerous. Firstly, its got some pretty smart styling, making the picture you load to edit look like it's on an easel. Down the side of the interface are the tools and options. The set up works in both landscape and portrait so you can adjust it according to the kind of picture you are editing. When you load a file from your library, you will find that it has been turned black and white, giving you the option of finger-painting the colour back into the picture. On top of

that simple system are a couple of other cool features that will enhance the treatment you can give your composition. The first is the mask tool, which can be used to more easily view the area you are going to colourise. You also have the option of using different sized brushes for more detailed work, and you can choose between a soft or hard brush to reveal colour in a more subtle or obvious way. With some practice, you can create some truly stunning pictures. This is a great, easy way to vamp-up your photos and the results are very rewarding. A very simple but effective app for those of a creative disposition.

Rating ★★★★☆

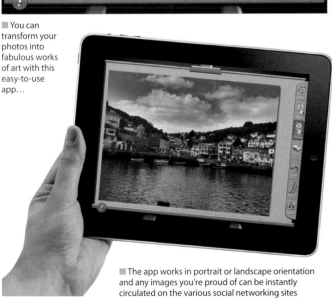

■ You can transform your photos into fabulous works of art with this easy-to-use app…

■ The app works in portrait or landscape orientation and any images you're proud of can be instantly circulated on the various social networking sites

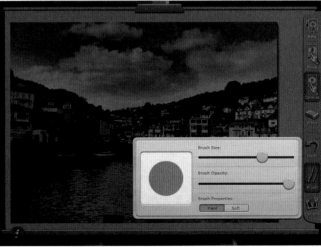

■ With a simple set of tools at your disposal you can mask certain areas of your picture and apply colour to other parts to lift it

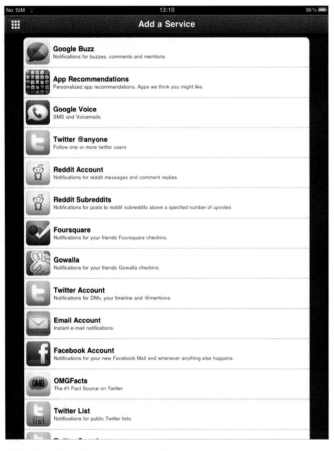

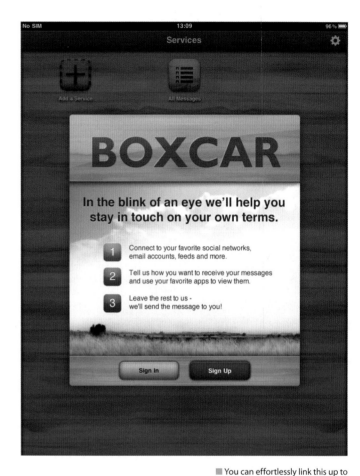

Price: Free **Developer:** Jonathan George

You can effortlessly link this up to Twitter and other sites to get all your feeds in one handy hit

Boxcar The news not when it happens, but as it happens…

Oddly, if you've no friends in this world whatsoever, Boxcar is certainly the app for you – though we sincerely doubt that was Jonathan George's intention in creating it.

More central to its existence is the plethora of social networking options available online nowadays. Whether it's through Twitter, Facebook, Foursquare, Google Buzz or any other portal, there's no shortage of places to keep up with current events of a serious or comedic nature. Trouble is, having so many sources can lead to mass confusion amid the bundles of data being cleaved out of the internet and thrown in the unsuspecting user's direction each day.

Boxcar effectively addresses this situation by breaking down each of the above providers – along with email and RSS feeds – offering push notifications to your Apple device throughout the day the very instant one person or outlet updates. Rather than having to scroll through perhaps hundreds of Twitter feeds, or the brain-dead output of Facebook friends whose only concern is their next binge drinking session, it is now possible to cherry-pick the most valuable contacts across all fields, and be updated on them instantly.

What's more, with specific relevance to Twitter, if you're interested in all the members of a particular band, magazine team or perhaps newsroom, the app makes slotting all of their tweets together into an easily distinguishable whole just that little bit easier. It'll also open your preferred Twitter client, should you dislike Boxcar's own interface for any particular reason. Naturally, if the idea of receiving push notifications every time an acquaintance has breakfast seems like some sort of living hell, rest assured you can restrict the app's functionality to certain times (though sadly not days of the week).

The app did seem a little too prone to crashing upon various commands for our liking though, and this otherwise generous gesture does rely upon advertising support to survive (unless you're okay with the £4.99/$9.99 ad removal fee), but there's little denying Boxcar's streamlining functions are pretty useful in this multi-multimedia world. Essential programming for the social network user who loves to network just that little bit too much.

Rating ★★★★☆

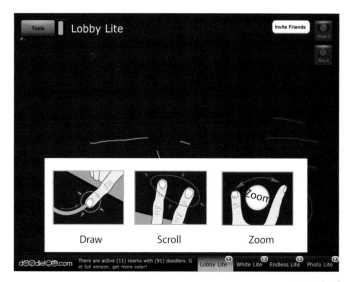

Price: Free **Developer:** DoodleToo

DoodleToo Lite

Bring out the artist in you

As jaw-dropping social network apps go, this has to rank right near the top. We were presented with a blank screen and little idea of what we were supposed to do. So we scrawled a few lines. The next thing, something else was being drawn, accompanied by the word 'guest'. Someone who we have never met was doodling with us, and it was quite astonishing.

The app has two versions: a paid-for one a free one. And the free version suited us fine for what we wanted to do, which was play and interact (the full has more rooms, colour and better social facilities). You can invite friends to join you so that you're not randomly drawing with strangers and you can also snap your creation and send it via email or on Facebook, adding a message while you're at it.

DoodleToo Lite has a number of 'rooms' which offer various backdrops (the Photo Lite room, for example, has some scenic shots and White Lite is, as you would expect, just a plain white background). You can browse these, either looking for playmates or to find a different vibe. And if you want to communicate with anyone, you just tap 'Say It' and you have 120 characters for your message. It's great fun to use and well worth installing on your device.

■ Some brief instructions are provided but it's all about the experience

Rating ★★★★★

"You can invite friends to join you so that you're not drawing with strangers"

Price: Free **Developer:** Osmosis Apps Limited

Tap to Chat 2 for Facebook Chat

Chat while you surf the net

One of the most popular aspects of social-networking site Facebook, besides the status updates, is the chat facility. Tap to Chat 2 draws this one particular feature out and wraps a standalone app around it, making it easier to converse with friends who happen to be online.

As soon as you log on using your Facebook details, the app will scour your account for any friends who happen to be online. So with this app, there is no need to jump to people's profiles and no messing around with tiny boxes on desktops. Once you're presented with your available friend, you can chat with one or more of them.

Although there is a separate app for GoogleTalk, it would be nice if these facilities were included in the one app for a better, more rounded experience. But that's not to say that Tap to Chat 2 is any less of an app for concentrating on one chat facility at a time.

You can change your status from Online to Offline, Away or Invisible if you wish and you can toggle the sound effects and background alerts. The text can be enlarged if you wish it to be bigger. Finally, the app also runs on the iPhone and the iPod touch.

Rating ★★★★★

■ Tap to Chat has a host of options and you can even share news of the app

■ The app searches for friends and, if there are none, displays this clearly

Apps

Price: Free **Developer:** TripTrace

Pingster Be famous for 15 minutes

Pingster presents you with a big red button and, when you tap it, you will become visible to anyone else using the app within your vicinity. You remain visible for 15 minutes, during which time people are able to locate you and attempt to contact you if they wish.

This may seem like a stalker's paradise but the key is that everyone remains anonymous, with only usernames visible to other people. You can probably see one flaw – you only get to see people if they are logged in and they have pressed the button too and so, like many social networks, it really does depend on the number of people who not only download it but use it as well.

But it's a very easy app to use. You can view a map to see exactly where you are on it and you can create emails and hook into Facebook as all social network apps worth their salt now do. Overall, it's an ambitious app that aims to connect people in real life using virtual means and without attempting to compromise your identity or safety.

■ You can see where you are on the in-built map

Rating ★★★★★

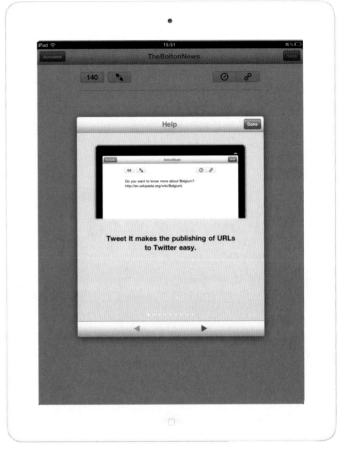

Price: £1.49/$0.99 **Developer:** Andre Williams

Tweet It It's yet another Twitter app

If you've ever used the brilliant iA Writer app, which aims to make word processing a far simpler affair, then you will take to Tweet It like a duck to water. The app strips away all but the ability to create a status update, which is mightily refreshing and also means you are going to be tweeting far more in the weeks and months to come.

The main screen is simply white. You can type your 140 characters into it and then press Send and, given that you have linked a Twitter account to it, it will show in your feed. You can have more than one account too.

But it's not just a matter of writing a status and sending it. You will want more than that for your money. So Tweet It adds a few extra handy features such as a link to a web browser so that you can quickly find an internet address and cut and paste it into your tweet with just a couple of taps. And you can shorten web addresses by pressing the option to make it a bit.ly address.

If you have already been surfing the web and come across something worth tweeting, the app will pick up the last URL you were on before you opened Tweet It so you can effortlessly paste it in.

Rating ★★★★★

Price: £2.99/$2.99 **Developer:** Fomola

Blogsy

iPad blogging made easy?

Blogging is currently one of the world's most popular technological hobbies – and has been for quite some time – with many ordinary people providing larger-than-140-character updates on how their life is going mixed in with inane and sometimes slightly disturbing rants. So it makes sense that purpose-built blogging iPad apps such as Blogsy exist.

When you first start the app up, you are greeted with what could well be considered a rarity in the App Store: a genuinely helpful welcome/tutorial page, which gives you all you need to start posting to your WordPress or Google Blogger blogs. It goes into great detail about how you work the main mechanics of Blogsy, and by making it the first thing you see, you have no excuse not to know how the app works.

The first thing to note – and, indeed, the main gist of the aforementioned tutorial – is that the app has two 'sides' to it: the Rich Side and the Write Side, and throughout your blog editing/writing with Blogsy you will probably be using both in equal measure. The Write Side is by far the more technical of the two – it's essentially an HTML version of your blog's content – and, as the name suggests, it's where you write the blog. Of course, you use the iPad's on-screen keyboard to enter data, and as usual the dreaded autocorrect is in full effect here, so be careful! If you don't catch your potentially embarrassing

and costly mistake early, you may fall victim to one of Blogsy's most annoying problems.

Fomola has designed its app so you simply switch from Rich to Write side with a horizontal swish of your finger. It's a great idea in theory, but you do a similar gesture when selecting the incorrect text, meaning that Blogsy will shift modes when you're trying to change a mistake – it's infuriating at best.

The Rich Side is where you can see how your blog entry looks so far, and take advantage of the app's best feature: integration. Blogsy allows files from Flickr, Picasa, YouTube and Google. Accounts are needed for all (except for Google that is), but if you have access to these sites, then Blogsy makes it very easy to use this content – it's just a case of dragging the video/image you want, and placing it into your blog. We would like to see some music sites supported, but these will doubtless come from future updates.

It's definitely let down by a few almost fundamental control issues, but Blogsy is a decent blogging app with some potential. We recommend keeping an eye out for future updates.

Rating ★★★☆☆

■ The app's design is rather sparse, but this just gives you maximum room to blog

■ The multimedia options are decent, and you can attach YouTube videos

Apps

Price: Free **Developer:** Eurosport

Eurosport for iPad

Sports coverage from across Europe with all the latest news

Eurosport has done a great job of covering the less glamorous sports and catering for live events other than football since its inception. This iPad app doesn't include all of those same fringe sports, but there's no denying that there is a good selection of coverage.

There is a large choice of news, league standings and latest results from all over Europe. Those whose interests lie outside the Premiership and UK football leagues will find loads of results and news from Germany, Italy and Spain, not to mention other worldwide sports leagues too.

The interface is a bit busy and the way the breaking news sections and live sport results panes whizz back and forth is a touch unsettling. We like the way you can change the size of the text and even the font if you prefer, to tailor the app to your preferences. There are also handy share on Facebook or send by email options from within the app. The Eurosport app is great and has the added benefit of being free, but we'd have liked to see some video included and the layout could do with some polish.

Rating ★★★★☆

■ The Eurosport app shows you an incredible range of sporting news though the layout could do with some polish

■ You can see breaking news from sports leagues all over the world

Price: Free **Developer:** DBG World LTD

Hayemaker

The app for your favourite fighter

This app is for fans of David Haye and although – as one would expect – the information and news centres around him, there is a fair smattering of other interesting boxing news. It's interesting to get the opinion of the heavyweight fighter in the blog section of the app and this does bring an added touch of personality to this tidy looking boxing app.

The Q&A section is also definitely worth a look. Here you can get an insight onto what the fans want to know and what David Haye is prepared to reveal. Some of the answers were disappointingly short and left you wanting a bit more meat to get your teeth into, but others were actually very insightful. If you are a real fan of his you'll no doubt enjoy them all.

As an app, it's nicely designed with some slick elements. We were impressed that it was free but don't worry, they've managed to sneak a David Haye Store into the mix so you can part with some cash if you really want to. If you are a boxing fan or just David Haye fan, this is worthy of an install for sure. It's just a shame the man himself has decided to hang up his gloves.

Rating ★★★★☆

■ A simple clean interface makes the app easy to use and navigate

■ The app provides information about a number of David Haye's previous fights

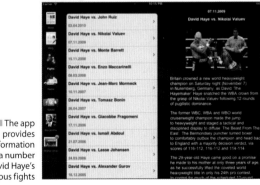

"It's nicely designed with some slick elements"

■ You have to be a subscriber to a Sky package to get video on the iPad

■ Picking a channel is simple, just tap on the one you want to watch and the line-up is displayed on the right

■ Get the ball to the front man. There you go, lesson over

■ The app is designed to help with all sports

Price: Free (app requires Sky subscription)   **Developer:** BSkyB

Sky Go

Watch the very best sports and Sky coverage wherever you are

You can't always be in front of a TV when the sports action is taking place so Sky has put its sports channels on the iPad for mobile viewing.

The app is a free download for anyone with a Sky Sports 1 and 2 subscription. The app itself can be loaded onto two iDevices, but is only compatible with iOS 4.2 and upwards. It allows you to watch all five Sky Sports channels for free while away from your TV, and as an added bonus anyone who also has a subscription to Sky Movies 1 and 2 can access a range of film channels for free as well. There's no doubt then that Sky is offering up some of its big hitters here.

The app works well and is definitely a handy app for people with all the necessary subscriptions. There have been some reports of a few compatibility issues and slow loading times, and it would be nice to have a few more channels available. However, the interface is easy to use and in our experience everything worked as expected.

We found this app to be a very nice extension to your Sky subscription package, and if you often find yourself missing sport events or your favourite shows then this could certainly be worth a download, especially as it's free.

Rating ★★★☆☆

Price: £2.99/$4.99   **Developer:** AlphaSprite Limited

CoachPad

Tips and tactics to manage a better team

If you've ever fancied yourself as a football manager, play in a local sports team or just love discussing sports strategies with your mates then you're bound to be interested in this useful little app. CoachPad presents you with blank layouts of a number of different sports, ranging from football to basketball and tennis. Once you've chosen the template you wish to use it's possible to sketch all manner of different plays and formations on it.

Useful items ranging from different coloured pens to line tools and ball tokens are all available, you can choose from a variety of different icons to reflect balls and other sports tools and it's relatively easy to drag on-screen items over to new locations in order to better show off chosen tactics. You can go online to download additional templates, import backdrops and, best of all, link up to a larger screen to show off all of your final plans.

Despite its overall versatility, CoachPad is far from perfect. The inability to draw new plans while linked to a bigger screen frustrates, which is a shame as this is otherwise good.

Rating ★★★☆☆

■ The videos will get you below par, but their quality is anything but

 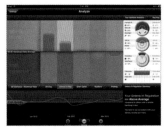

Price: £2.99/$4.99 **Developer:** Shotzoom Software, LLC

Golfplan

A professional app for golfers with professional aspirations

 Golfplan With Paul Azinger is a wonderfully well-crafted golfing app that means business. It has links to Golfshot accounts, so if you've already invested time in that system you can use this one too. You can also download the Golfshot app (although it's somewhat more expensive at a massive £20.99!) and the two will communicate to offer you the details of your swing and other training elements you've participated in.

But back to this app, and the instructional videos it contains are worth the already cheap cover price. They are very well shot, expertly delivered and will help you get to grips with a number of common techniques that most golfers crave the answers to. You can download more videos from within the app for free and of course there are a number of in-app purchases too. If you are seriously into golf, beyond just popping down the pitch and putt, then this app is an exceptional example of great content being offered at a great price. A worthy instructional app for players of all abilities.

Rating ★★★★☆

Price: £0.69/$0.99 **Developer:** Stephen Reynold

Football Rumours

Don't flick to the back pages – this app will deliver all the gossip

 If you're a big football fan, the close season that runs from June until the middle of August presents a time where each and every story that is presented in the papers and on the TV – whether it is true or not – could seriously change the fortunes of your team as they prepare for the next season.

So to get your rumour fix, you could read a load of newspapers, visit a ton of websites and watch the same news reports all day long – or you could let the Football Rumours app do all of the hard work for you. Of course all the bigger teams get all the gossip – which is true of the papers and the websites, to be honest – but there is still a massive amount of content here, as there should be. And it's not just a boring RSS ticker.

You can of course filter the result so that you get just the news from your own club, but you may find that this filters too much and you're not getting your money's worth, even though you've only paid £0.69/$0.99. Besides, if you want to keep up with the banter you need to know what's going on with your rivals too.

Rating
★★★★☆

■ Get links to full articles that offer more detail

■ Easy-to-read updates come thick and fast every day

Apps

Price: Free Developer: iQuest Technologies

Trip Viewer Bring your holidays to life

Once upon a time, people would invite others around to view their holiday slideshows and flick through photos. Then folks had video parties, showing off their latest camcorder escapades in a caravan park. But these 'experiences' are nothing when compared to the interactive way people can view your trips on the iPad with this new app.

iQuest Technologies' Trip Viewer lets you chart a route through your holiday destination, adding images and video to maps. It works in combination with the Trip Journal app on the iPhone or

> "Tapping on the notes option brings up info that's taken from Wikipedia"

Android, enabling you to import any trips you have documented on your handset. The Trip Viewer app then plots your route and includes all of the multimedia content for each specific location.

So if you took many images of New York outside the Empire State Building, tapping on that location will show up the variety of pictures as well as any video you may have gathered. But that's not all. If you tap the Play function in the top-right-hand corner of the iPad display, it will take you on an air balloon ride through the location.

As the balloon passes over area of key interest, it will display your photos in a slideshow before moving on to the next set of images. Images show up as green blobs on the map and videos are blue. By tapping on an image, you can see them in a larger size and you can use your fingers to zoom in. Beneath the image is a selection of other photos which can also be tapped and viewed.

Tapping on the notes option brings up information that has been taken from Wikipedia. So, you may be in the vicinity of the Eiffel Tower within the app. You can view the images and any video, but also tap the notes icon and find out more about it.

What Trip Viewer does is bring a destination to life and, more importantly, it shows your perspective on it. With the ability to use Flickr photos in real-time, you can combine your experience with other people's. Not only can you then share your trips but see other's too, and you can do so in your own time and in comfort rather than feeling you have to gush when your friend is explaining the great time they had.

This is the first version of the app, which will surely only get even better as time goes on, and the fact that it is free is a bonus. Do be aware, however, that there is a cost for Trip Journal (£0.69/$0.99) but that's also worth the cost when you consider the package you have here.

Rating ★★★★★

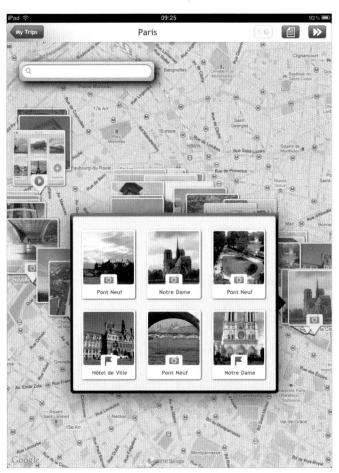

■ By tapping on an image, you can bring up your photos and view them neatly

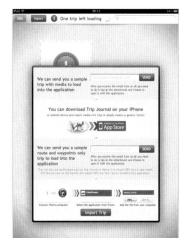

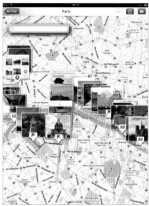

■ All of your images and video are displayed on a map so you can see where you have been

■ Trips can be imported from the Trip Viewer app on iPhone and Android

Apps

Price: Free **Developer:** Alan Paxton

The Complete National Cycle Network

It's time to get on your bike

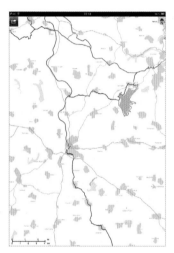

With more than 25,000 miles of cycle paths documented in this app, keen cyclists will certainly be overjoyed. It suggests recommended routes and is perfect for quiet Sunday afternoons or even trying to work out a better way through the hectic traffic on the way to work. You can even draw your own route on the map.

■ Suggested routes are shown on a map, which can be zoomed in

Rating ★★★★★

Price: Free **Developer:** TripTrace

mapOmatic

You'll never walk alone with this app

Ask mapOmatic for directions and it will draw the result on your own private map, storing it in your history folder for future use. It also hooks into Facebook and Foursquare, with a heart button showing all the places in your vicinity where your friends have checked in, meaning you could hotfoot it to where they are for an impromptu meet-up. The app also smoothly integrates with Pingster.

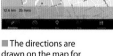
■ The directions are drawn on the map for you, and they're stored in your history

Rating ★★★★☆

Price: Free **Developer:** Pear Logic

Maps+

Taking mapping to another level

This app's free but it does have limitations. You can only place pins on the map a limited number of times; if you want more, you must pay £1.99/$2.99 for unlimited access. Is it worth it? Well, Maps+ takes the traditional Google map and extends its capabilities. It searches for local tweets, lets you track your location, and it can set location-specific alarms.

■ You can set an alarm for a specific location

Rating ★★★★☆

Price: £0.69/$0.99 **Developer:** Piet Jones

Speed App

Avoid getting an accidental ticket

Roads today have many speed cameras, and we all know it's very easy to find your foot pressing on the accelerator without realising and just accidentally edging over the speed limit. With Speed App in your car, you can see just how fast you're going at all times, either in mph or kph. While you may think you have this facility on the dashboard of your car, what the app does is change colour when you go at a certain speed. So you can see out of the corner of your eye if you are going too fast.

■ The colour changes depending on your speed

Rating ★★★☆☆

Price: £10.49/$14.99 **Developer:** Tamajii Inc

Storyboards Premium

With this scene-crafting iPad app, Hollywood's red carpet starts at the tips of your fingers...

Storyboards Premium offers self-explanatory help to budding writers, comic-book creators and movie directors in order for them to form a more clear picture in their mind of a narrative before committing it to paper, or indeed celluloid. Unlike its free counterpart, this paid-for edition allows a whole manner of techniques to be employed, smoothing the transition from the artist's initial conception though to the final product. Though some additional functionality is left to be desired, such features would tread on the toes of regular image manipulation software were they to be included, meaning that expert users may well wish to become familiar with an app of that kind before putting Storyboards Premium to active use. Amateurs and professionals hoping to offer a brief narrative outline, though, should find the options on offer to be more than adequate.

Creator Tamajii allows users to create an unlimited number of storyboards, each composed of a theoretically infinite total of individual

"This is a lavishly produced and easy-to-use iPad app"

frames. After selecting an appropriate background (which could naturally feature a simply manipulated photo from your library), users are free to populate each panel with their choice of dozens of incidental objects, ranging from heavy goods vehicles and the humble club sandwich, to – naturally – human figures. Each on-screen actor can be customised via a simple single tap, switching between a handful of costume ideas and a rainbow of fabric colours. Naturally too, this principle cast can be rotated over eight compass directions, allowing users to expand and contract their size to be shown from every conventional camera angle. So, bad news if you like your actors shot from below through a sheet of glass. There's good news if you're the kind of individual that prizes ergonomics over finer details, though. Simpler panels can be completed in well under one minute, thanks in part to a handy ability to favourite items used with greater frequency.

Similarly to their human counterparts, each in-app prop can be rotated, scaled and made transparent to each user's content, allowing for swift placement of auxiliary objects inside a room, even at the last possible minute. Though pixel-perfect accuracy naturally isn't quite achievable with such a limited set of tools, especially given that the app won't permit figures to be cut out from pre-existing digital camera images, a rough approximation of the scene is always possible here. Though more artistic visionaries may feel the need to import background images drawn by their own hand, the level of integration on offer here makes an occasional painstaking frame more than worthwhile.

This is a lavishly produced and easy-to-use iPad app that is sure to inspire you to start mapping out your own movies.

Rating ★★★★☆

■ Objects can be scaled, rotated and placed within your scenes to help you visualise how each scene will look

■ The app is so easy to use that you'll be drafting out you own storyboards in minutes. But when do the cameras start rolling?

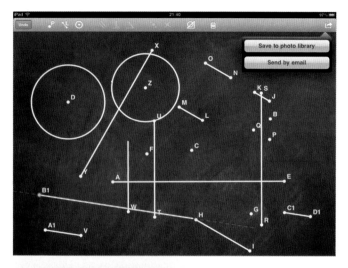

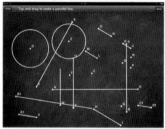

■ You simply move your finger around the slate to create perfect geometrical shapes in an instant

■ All that's missing is an option to instantly (and quite literally) wipe the slate clean

Price: £1.49/$1.99 **Developer:** zheng min Wei

GeoBoard

Geometry at your fingertips

 Being able to draw a perfect circle generally isn't a skill possessed by many people. Regular folk have to use a tool like a compass, but on GeoBoard you just need a single finger. Drag a fingertip across the blackboard-style screen, and it'll make a perfect circle appear precisely to the size you like. Why? Because GeoBoard is a drawing tool for nerds, allowing you to create all kinds of geometrical illustrations by hand. In addition to circles, they include straight, parallel and perpendicular lines. There's also the ability to draw a line at any angle you like relative to another point, the option to create a point exactly midway between two others, and slightly more complicated things we don't understand, like creating an intersection for lines and circles.

What's the use of all this? As mere intellectual mortals, we're not really sure, but GeoBoard seems to be only suited to geometry students or teachers, and is very popular with said users if the user reviews are anything to go by. Without that specialist knowledge, all we can say is that GeoBoard is a smart and well-made app, albeit one for a very specialist field.

Rating ★★★★☆

Price: £1.99/$2.99 **Developer:** Fabrication Games

Mannequin

Strike a pose with this virtual 3D artist's mannequin

 On the face of it, the app is a simple and straightforward: there is a plain textured background, a fully poseable 3D figure, and a modest array of controls. However, it is the 3D lay figure that holds the interest. It's fully controllable using an array of finger gestures. Users can take any joint and twist and bend into the desired position, turn the model in various directions and rotate 360 degrees. In fact, the figure can be manoeuvred into almost any position simply using swipes, taps and gestures. It is worth noting that there is no way to save poses, and no zoom.

Beyond finger control, the app has a host of buttons and sliders to get more precise positioning. There is a chain function which allows users to move whole limbs in unison or at least more than one part together. Tap to switch off and each individual element is free to move.

More recent additions to the app include a very useful reset button that takes the 3D figure back to its original state. For those feeling uninspired there is the random pose button and for those who have made a wrong move there is an undo and redo button to save the day. The ideal app for budding artists, a lay figure that fits in a pocket or bag. It certainly won't interest everyone, but still worth a look.

Rating ★★★☆☆

■ Move him how you like and then tap a button to reset his position

■ This is perhaps only really of interest to artists and animators

GoodNotes

Price: £2.49/$2.99 **Developer:** Time Base Technology Limited

If you're not a fan of keyboards, this does the job

GoodNotes lets you use your finger or a stylus to add notes to pages. It gives you control over the scale of the notes so you can write big letters or cram in small print, and also choose the thickness of your pen. You have the choice of paper types, and can re-arrange pages and projects with the utmost ease. What's more, you can add a wrist rest so that you don't accidentally add random inputs.

In practice, this app is mildly useful. If you have a decent stylus, then it's a completely different app. It's controlled, easy to use, and lot more effective. In terms of build and ease of use, this app trumps many more expensive note-taking apps that are available. Its excellent instructions see to it you know exactly what to do once it's downloaded. An enjoyably simple notes app that's best suited to use with a stylus. Without one, it's only average, so it may be worth considering a purchase quite carefully.

■ You basically use your finger as a stylus to draw on the screen. Basic stuff, but it works

Rating
★★★★☆

Price: Free **Developer:** Addition, Lda

I'm Downloading

Offering you all the downloads and links that you could possibly want

One of the major complaints about the iPad as a viable replacement for a desktop computer is that it doesn't have the file hierarchy to support normal computer behaviour online. This comes in many forms, one of them being an inability to download files from the web, as there is nowhere to put them.

Luckily, clever developers exist to think of ways around such problems. I'm Downloading offers a limited but useful option for those that wish to grab files from online and save them to the iPad. In most cases, the files you download aren't useable on the iPad, but they can be later transferred to a main computer through iTunes. The main element of the app is a browser where you can search for those files you want to download. You have the choice of search engines, and can of course go direct to a URL. Once you've got to a page that contains the download file, a message pops up once you tap the button, and your download is added to a queue. Once it's safely landed in the app, you can view it, save it and edit its name. It can then be exported during the next sync for proper use. A very well-made, easy-to-use app.

Rating

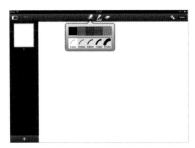

■ The main element of the app is a browser where you can search for files to download

■ Once in the app, you can view the file, save it and edit the name

Price: £6.99/$9.99 Developer: Aji, LLC

iAnnotate PDF

Mark-up and edit your files

iAnnotate PDF is a handy tool that allows you to mark up and edit standard PDF files on your iPad. There are a full range of tools available that enable you to highlight elements, cross out text and even add your own comments to the PDFs themselves.

The range of options is really flexible and the annotations that we tested worked exactly as expected when opened on Macs and PCs – in both Preview on the Mac and Adobe Reader on the PC. Annotating PDFs is one of those tasks that seems built around a mouse and keyboard, but iAnnotate really does make it possible to annotate a PDF on the touch screen of the iPad.

Each PDF opens in a tab, enabling you to quickly jump between documents. You can also email annotated PDFs from within the app, so it's a fully featured tool that's perfect when you're on the move. For £6.99 this is a great app and if you annotate PDFs on a regular basis it'll soon become indispensable.

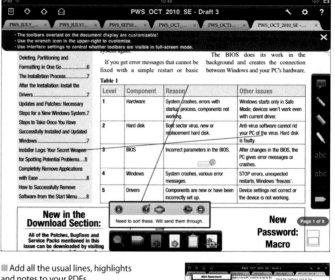

■ Add all the usual lines, highlights and notes to your PDFs…

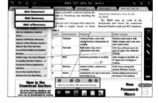

■ You can mail your marked PDFs directly from the app…

Rating ★★★★★

Dropbox Online storage, and all for free!

Price: Free Developer: Dropbox

Unfortunately the iPad doesn't actually have a built-in file manager and therefore it can be a bit of a pain to transfer your files to it from a computer. It means that you have to open iTunes and manually drag files across, then sync to get them onto your iPad.

Dropbox for iPad integrates with the free online storage service of the same name to give you a better method of managing your files. It's not quite a fully fledged file manager, but it allows you to easily use documents on your iPad. Dropbox gives you 2GB of free online storage and you can copy any file that the iPad understands to the service. Open Dropbox for iPad and you can see all the files and use them as you wish. You can even stream video content too.

With many other iPad apps allowing you to save to or read from your Dropbox, it's a great tool for managing documents. For a free app, Dropbox is excellent and getting 2GB of free online storage is great too. If you need more space, you can upgrade to 50GB or 100GB options.

■ Store and open all sorts of file types

Rating ★★★★★

Apps

Speak It! Text To Speech
Price: £1.49/$1.99 **Developer:** John Stefanopolos

Make talking that little bit cheaper

■ Emailed sound files are sent directly from the app itself

We suppose many aspects of modern life would have astounded us, ten or 20 years ago. Live online gaming, for instance, or how terribly expensive things are. Topping the list, though, come apps like Speak It!, which allows a device in the palm of your hand to speak for itself near-perfectly.

It's not quite as simple as that, naturally. Though its sales blurb suggests the ability to read PDF files, it can only do this insofar as it can read any copied and pasted text from any document. So, before having the device spell out any text, users must delve into the source document as they would have done anyway, which is a shame but doesn't kill off the app's purpose entirely.

It's possible, for instance, to send a spoken message to others via email, just through the entry of text. Naturally, too, it may prove of use to those unwilling to strain their eyes through the viewing of large text documents to have one of this app's four automatons speak it to them while either browsing other apps or doing nothing at all. The interface isn't great but this is still a triumph.

Rating ★★★★☆

Verto Studio 3D
Price: £9.99/$7.99 **Developer:** Michael Farrell

A new 3D design studio that's heading in the right direction

Verto Studio 3D is, in essence, a sandbox design studio that intends to replicate what other programs already offer on the PC. It brings a whole new level of functionality to an otherwise untapped market, but – as is the case with new apps – there are teething issues which need to be ironed out. The first thing that's apparent when loading up a new document is the amount of options that are available. Although it's fairly cheap, the developer really hasn't held back. There's a sizeable array of texture mapping and editing tools, from 360 degree camera control to individual object mesh manipulation. You can import your own textures and objects, or use the stock ones available, all performed with a user-friendly interface and some basic touch screen controls.

Once in a scene, the app runs smoothly for the most part, and editing or moving the scenery is a breeze. The utilities available for object editing purposes are considerable, but no doubt some designers will be left wanting more options in future versions. A great starting point but it needs a few tweaks if it is to ever be deemed an essential app.

Rating ★★★★☆

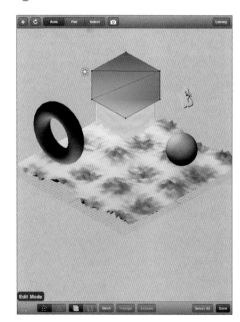

■ The developer certainly hasn't held back on the amount of options available…

■ There's a sizeable array of texture mapping and editing tools…

iPad Tips, Tricks, Apps and Hacks **175**